GIFTS
from the Hearth

Your Guide to the
Art of Hospitality

Elizabeth R. Skoglund

Discovery House Publishers is affiliated with RBC Ministries,
Grand Rapids, Michigan, 49512.
All rights reserved.

Discovery House books are distributed to the trade exclusively by Barbour
Publishing, Inc., Uhrichsville, Ohio 44683.

Unless otherwise noted, Scripture quotations are taken from
The Living Bible, © 1971 owned by assignment by
KNT Charitable Trust. All rights reserved. Verses marked KJV
are taken from the Holy Bible, King James Version.

Interior design by Sherri L. Hoffman

Library of Congress Cataloging-in-Publication Data

Skoglund, Elizabeth.
  Gifts from the hearth : your guide to the art of hospitality / Elizabeth R.
Skoglund.
    p.   cm.
  Includes bibliographical references and index.
    ISBN 1-57293-094-2
  1. Hospitality—Religious aspects—Christianity. 2. Hospitality—Biblical
teaching. 3. Cookery. I. Title.
BV4647.H67 S558 2003
241'.671—dc21   2002152914

Printed in the United States of America
03 04 05 06 07 08 09 / DP / 10 9 8 7 6 5 4 3 2 1

To Rayne, Lance, and Elizabeth Hannah
with gratitude for their contributions to the
hospitality of this home and to the writing of this
book. They will, I know, continue these traditions
and add to them in their own home, with their
family and friends, as well as in ministering
to the stranger at the gate.

❧ CONTENTS

 FOREWORD

A"ministry to others"—although this phrase does not occur until well into the body of this wonderful book, it is clearly the engine that drives Ms. Skoglund's commitment to hospitality. For her, hospitality is a "divine command." Reminiscent of Saint Paul's description of himself as becoming all things to all men, she very sensitively describes a huge range of approaches to hospitality—from the very formal to the casual—but always the message to the recipients of her hospitality is, "You are loved, you are important to me," as she seeks to create a "safe place" for her guests, where they and their burdens can be separated. She also shows that hospitality may sometimes be very costly—even to the point of laying down one's life.

Although many of her forays into hospitality seemed (and, in truth, were) spontaneous, they often worked only because of careful forward planning and organization—having pre-cooked dishes in the freezer, or recipes for apparently complex dishes which were readily assembled at short notice.

Elegance, simplicity, and meticulous thought all come together in her smorgasbord of wise counsel. Those who excel in conversation should not dwell overlong in the kitchen stirring soup! As a recipient of her hospitality on numerous occasions, this reviewer gladly attests to the fact that she practices what she preaches.

A host of wonderful recipes (beyond the competence of this reviewer to assess) accompany this invaluable book, which meets a sore need of life in America of the twenty-first century.

Matthew E. Conolly, M.D., F.A.C.P., F.R.C.P.
PROFESSOR OF MEDICINE, UCLA

❦ INTRODUCTION

Hospitality is a tradition that is added to and passed down from one generation to another, so writing a book about the comfort of the hearth has involved going back into my own roots, to people and places long gone. My maternal grandparents, Alfred and Carolina Benson, were Swedish immigrants who established a safety zone of hospitality in their home in Wisconsin, where they welcomed and ministered to everyone from Indians who still inhabited the area to itinerant pastors and family members from Chicago. That tradition was passed down to my mother and blended by marriage with the customs my father brought to their newly established home from his own immigrant past. My heritage has been enriched by friends also, forming a curious blend of Swedish, British, Chinese, and American, until my concept of hospitality has emerged as uniquely my own.

Throughout the text you will find certain recipes marked by a special icon, indicating that they can be found in a recipe section at the end of the book, along with practical helps and food facts. Remember, too, that the placement of a recipe in one chapter does not limit its appropriateness to that one type of event. For example, certain cookies can be used for Christmas, but also for picnics and teas. Scones are an example of simplicity, but can be equally effective when served for a tea.

All of the people who influenced this book cannot possibly be specifically recognized. But I am very grateful to have come from a family who offered hospitality to the stranger at the gate as well as their own friends and families, and I appreciate those among my family and friends who even now offer gifts from the hearth.

Special thanks go to my littlest helper, Elizabeth Hannah, and to Rayne and Lance Wilcox, who helped with typing, food tasting—and testing—as well as sorting through ideas for this book. My thanks to to Mitchell Davis of The James Beard Foundation who took time during the holiday season to answer questions in a thoughtful and precise way. Special gratitude goes to Steve Nevens who tested and retested the use of pasteurized eggs and actually introduced me to Davidson's pasteurized eggs. Thanks, too, go to James Sluss, Director of Sales Planning for Pasteurized Eggs Corporation, who shared important current information regarding salmonella and eggs and referred me to available resources.

Few publishers are as pleasant to work with as Discovery House. My thanks go to publisher Carol Holquist for her creative ideas, Judith Markham for her editorial support and organizational skills, Kim Collins for her insight into promotion, and Beth Koops, who is a valuable resource for various types of information. Thanks also to Tim Gustafson who was there at the start and once again at the end.

The gifts from the hearth that we offer to each other on this earth are just a foretaste of the abundant hearth we shall share someday in eternity, where our Lord will preside and we shall partake together in that place of comfort and safety.

The wayfarers come to us continually, and they do not come by chance. God sends them. And as they come ... they are our judges. Not merely by whether we give, but by how we give and by what we give, they judge us. ... Thank God there are some men and women here and there, full of the power of the Gospel, who cannot rest satisfied till they have opened their very hearts and given the poor wayfaring men the only thing which really is their own, themselves, their faith, their energy, their hope in God.

PHILLIPS BROOKS

That Means She Loves Us

A little girl was visiting her grandmother. Accustomed to fast food and hastily eaten dinners served on TV trays or in the back seat of a car, she stood mesmerized, looking at the sparkling crystal, the colorful china, and the silver cutlery.

Turning to her father, who was sitting across the room, she whispered loudly: "Come and look at this, Daddy."

Her father came. A little confused at the interruption for what seemed to him to be nothing, he asked, "What's wrong?"

"Look," she repeated, pointing proudly at the shiny silver cutlery and the sparkling cut-glass serving dish. "That means she loves us," she declared with certainty.

Later, as I watched the child eating contentedly, with a formality of manners consistent with the importance of the occasion in her mind, I realized even more completely how much the extra details of hospitality can communicate love.

I remembered a scene many years earlier, when I was a small child seated at another table and another meal, this time breakfast. It was early 1942. Pearl Harbor had been bombed. The United States was officially at war. There was talk about Japanese planes sighted off the coast of California, where we lived. As a result, windows were blacked out at night, and sirens often caught us unaware on the street.

There were economic restrictions, too. My parents were issued small books of food coupons that allowed them to buy only limited quantities of rationed items like meat, sugar, and coffee. Gasoline was rationed, but for the moment that didn't matter to us because we didn't have a car yet. We had just moved to California the year before so that my father could design planes for Lockheed Aircraft. Now, with the declaration of war between us and Germany as well as Japan, his work carried more personal significance, which also made all of us more acutely aware of the war than we might have been otherwise.

On this particular Monday morning, the discussion around the breakfast table was not focused on war, or the car my father was soon to buy, or even the house to which we were shortly to move. On this spring morning the topic was sugar, and at the moment it seemed all-important. Breakfast turned into a democratic caucus convened to decide one vital question: How should the week's small allotment of sugar be used? The choice basically came down to two possibilities: a week of sugar with coffee for the adults—or a cake at the end of the week, which could be shared with us children.

I remember the debate. I remember the decision: cake at the end of the week. And I remember feeling loved; for even at that age I knew that in any good Swedish household, coffee—with its cream and sugar—was valued above any cake. But that week my parents showed their love for my sister and me by giving up the sugar in their coffee. Like the significance of crystal, china, and silver to the five-year-old at her grandmother's house, the adult decision to give up sugar, some fifty years ago, meant to two other children, born in a different time, that we, too, were loved.

In a world threatened by the horrors of world war, the "safety zone" of a home that offered hospitality, first to its own family and then to others, buffered the coldness and danger in the world outside. It provided an antidote for loneliness. Cake for Sunday dinner was something to look forward to; and as such, it was a small symbol of permanence that could be counted on in the middle of a world of impermanence.

Well over half a century later the world is threatened by another war, a new kind of war: international terrorism. Unfortunately, terrorism has existed for years in many parts of the world, but since September 11, 2001, it has become a vivid reality here in America. For all of us, life has changed in many ways, large and small. We have terrorist alerts, rated on an imminent danger scale; endless searches in airports; school "lock downs," just in case; irradiated mail; and the news is filled daily with reports on "weapons of mass destruction," anthrax, biological and chemical warfare, and suicide bombers.

In the midst of this, all of us—children and adults—need to feel just a little more special than usual, just a little safer. Hospitality and home are important again, not so much as showcases of affluence, but as places of safety and love. Family is important. "Home-cooked food" and "comfort food" are terms we hear more often now. We cling to the good memories of the past, which are often connected with food, and we talk about "making memories" for our children. Cozy and intimate are "in" for people of all ages.

WHAT IS HOSPITALITY? 🌿

One of the most elaborate dinner parties I ever went to was served in a lovely, large, formal dining room. The food was exotic and was perfectly arranged on striking black-and-white plates. The table was decorated in black and white, with an emphasis on geometric shapes for the napkin rings, candleholders, and centerpiece of white flowers.

In the background played some rather monotonous music. At the table itself a stiff, awkward conversation started and stopped at regular intervals. I put in my time until it was appropriate to leave. Once outside in the cool night air, I felt as though I had regained my freedom. I would have traded that dinner party in a minute for porridge by someone's warm, friendly fire!

In contrast, true hospitality has the feeling of the hearth. It stands in opposition to the coldness and depersonalization of the world outside. It provides a temporary respite that remains in the memory and refurbishes long after it is past. True hospitality is so important that the writer to the Hebrews warns us, "Never forget to be hospitable, for by hospitality some have entertained angels unawares."[1] H. C. G. Moule said of this passage:

> Dear to the heart of the believing Church for ages have been these precepts to love the brethren, to love the stranger, to remember Abraham at Mamre and Gideon at Ophrah with their angel-guests, and to see a possible angel-visitor in every needing stranger at the door.... The call ... to remember the captive, and the sufferer of every sort, comes with solemn power from this paragraph, as it presses home the law of sympathetic fellowship.

Hospitality is a gift. It is a gift that says to the person to whom it is given, "I care about you."

After leading the courageous rescue of 100,000 Jews in Budapest at the end of World War II, Swedish diplomat Raoul Wallenberg was captured by the Russians. One day another prisoner was put into Wallenberg's cell in the Gulag. Wallenberg was in solitary confinement, so the placement was a mistake and lasted for only a few hours.

Years later, when the prisoner was questioned in Stockholm regarding Wallenberg (who is still missing), he told the story about that day when he had been put in the prison cell. They had "talked" for the few hours they had, using prison sign language. But first Wallenberg had offered him half of his day's bread ration. When he was asked how he could be so sure of his memory after so many years, he replied that it was the only time in all of his years in the Gulag when someone had offered him part of his daily bread ration. Such love he could not forget. It was an act of the truest hospitality.

A hamburger given to a bag lady on a bus bench; an elaborate wedding dinner; a gift of firewood late at night from an innkeeper to someone just checking into a motel; a cool, wet towel given to someone at the scene of a car accident; a midnight snack shared with someone who needs to talk: all of these are acts of hospitality. They are gifts of love, freely given by one person to another. They are each a gift from the hearth. Each of these echoes the sentiment of the small child who said, "That means she loves us."

The place of hospitality will often be quite literally the welcoming hearth of one's home. But more fundamentally, it will always be the welcoming hearth of the heart. For while hospitality requires a physical place, it is even more essentially a place in the heart. Hospitality is the gift of oneself that says, "You are important; you are loved." ✣

We are never safe, but we have plenty of fun, and some ecstasy. It is not hard to see why. The security we crave would teach us to rest our hearts in this world and oppose an obstacle to our return to God: a few minutes of happy love, a landscape, a symphony, a merry meeting with our friends, a bath or a football match, have no such tendency. Our Father refreshes us on the journey with some pleasant inns, but will not encourage us to mistake them for home.

C. S. LEWIS

The Safety Zone of Hospitality

The year was 1936. The place was Chicago. My mother and father lived in an apartment building adjacent to one in which Aunt Esther and Uncle Blanton lived. The Great Depression was beginning to wind down; and unknown to most Americans, World War II was building up in Europe. Money was scarce, but my mother and her sister were blissfully happy in their roles as homemakers.

Neither my mother nor my aunt had a telephone back in those days. So every morning, after both husbands were off to work and their respective apartments had been tidied, Aunt Esther would put a pot of coffee on the stove. When it was ready, she would wave a white handkerchief in the window for my mother to see. It announced a mid-morning break of hospitality. It was the signal to my mother that said: "Coffee is ready. Come on over." It was a safety zone.

Each of us has places, people, things, activities, and beliefs that provide a buffer for us when life gets stressful and that help us refurbish our lives in order to go on. Each of us has safety zones already built into our lives. The familiar coffee shop with the friendly waitress; the favorite lines of an old hymn; routines, like Wednesday night prayer meeting at church or morning coffee at seven; an old friendship; a hobby, like gardening or stamp collecting: these are just a few of the thousands of potential safety zones that we all have and need. According to our own tastes and lifestyle, these safety zones vary from person to person and perhaps from year to year for any one person. Yet, while all of us have safety zones in our lives, most of us do not understand the nature of these safety zones; nor do we consciously use the concept of safety zones in order to improve our own lives and minister more effectively to others.

The most fundamental definition of a safety zone is that it is quite literally, a place of safety. During World War II, Le Chambon, a small village in the south of France, conspired to hide Jews and move them on to safety. Five thousand Gentiles saved five thousand Jews. Based on the idea of the Old Testament cities of refuge, each home fed, clothed, and protected anyone who knocked at its door, so "that innocent blood be not shed..." (Deuteronomy 19:10 KJV).

At the center of this activity was a pastor's wife who, while providing a place of physical safety for Jews, also offered the hospitality of a meal to Nazi agents who were her enemies and had, indeed, come to arrest her husband. Her reason? It was dinnertime, and she would have offered dinner to anyone who came at that time. She had an inner spirit of hospitality. Hospitality was a safety zone she offered to others.

Thus, even in the middle of offering places of literal safety, the sense of hospitality has to start from within. The act of hospitality is the outgrowth of an attitude. For those who protected Jews during the Holocaust, a Jewish proverb applies: "If you are in a place where there is no human being, be a human being."[1] In the middle of one of history's greatest examples of man's inhumanity to man, some became the exception. Some provided places of literal safety for those who were persecuted. Some exemplified the greatest sense of hospitality.

Madame Marie was a French woman who hid people in her apartment building. A modern Rahab, Madame Marie did a good job of diverting Nazi agents away from her building by deceptive statements that made them look elsewhere. One child she saved was Odette Meyers. According to her, "Madame Marie had a very simple philosophy. We were Jewish and she did not want to impose her religion on us, but she told me a story. 'The heart is like an apartment,' she said, 'and if it's messy and there is nothing to offer, no food or drink to offer guests, nobody will want to come. But if it's clean and dusted every day, and if it's pretty and there are flowers and food and drink for guests, people will want to come, and they will want to stay for dinner. And if it's super nice, God himself will want to come.'

"Whenever I would do something wrong, she would put me on a high stool facing the wall, and she would say to me, 'I think you have some housework to do.' It was my business to figure out how I had messed up my heart in some way. I had to get a broom and dustpan and get to work. That was her philosophy and what she taught me. It has been important all through my life."[2] The basis of any ministry of hospitality must start first from within the person.

WHAT IS A SAFETY ZONE? 🖋

Regardless of the specific gifts of any one person's hospitality, all hospitality should have the same end result: a safety zone of comfort, growth, and enjoyment. A number of years ago, the Little House books became famous again because of the long-running television series *Little House on the Prairie*. The warmth and wholesomeness that pervaded these books made people of all ages feel safe again. In *Little House in the Big Woods*, Laura Ingalls Wilder illustrates the safety-zone aspect of these stories when she describes an evening at home, with the warmth of the hearth in sharp contrast to the danger and chill outside:

> All alone in the wild Big Woods, and the snow, and the cold, the little log cabin was warm and snug and cosy. Pa and Ma and Mary and Laura and Baby Carrie were comfortable and happy there, especially at night.
>
> Then the fire was shining on the hearth, the cold and the dark and the wild beasts were all shut out, and Jack the brindle bulldog and Black Susan the cat lay blinking at the flames in the fireplace.
>
> Ma sat in her rocking chair, sewing by the light of the lamp on the table. The lamp was bright and shiny.... And then, Pa told stories.
>
> [One particular story was a scary one.] When Pa told this story, Laura and Mary shivered and snuggled closer to him. They were safe and snug on his knees, with his strong arms around them.
>
> They liked to be there, before the warm fire, with Black Susan purring on the hearth and good dog Jack stretched out beside her. When they heard a wolf howl, Jack's head lifted and the hairs stood stiff along his back. But Laura and Mary listened to that lonely sound in the dark and the cold of the Big Woods, and they were not afraid.
>
> They were cosy and comfortable in their little house made of logs, with the snow drifted around it and the wind crying because it could not get in by the fire.[3]

Today, in the twenty-first century, we fear nuclear annihilation, suicide bombers, and germ warfare more than we fear wolves at the door. Mass communication exposes us to more bloodshed and violence in one day than our ancestors saw in years. We face medical testing that may show us not only what diseases we have, but those we are likely to get, without necessarily offering a cure. With our potential life span doubled since the turn of the last century, we look forward to old age; at the same time we talk about our right to once again shorten that life span through euthanasia and assisted suicide. We watch animals become extinct, and we revel in green plants and clear brooks because we know they are becoming a rarity.

The dangers that threaten us are not as simple as those the inhabitants of a log cabin encountered over a hundred years ago. In our day-to-day life we are probably safer than our ancestors on the prairie were, but the long-range dangers that threaten us are more frightening because we have so little control over them. At no time in the history of mankind has it felt more necessary to trust in the loving sovereignty of God. At no time have we more desperately needed to hear the words of the Scriptures: "You are safe in the care of the Lord your God, just as though you were safe inside his purse!" (1 Samuel 25:29).

This is our place in history, and it is in this place that we must live out the biblical command to be given to hospitality. It is a unique call for each of us, given at a unique time in the history of mankind, to share in the work of our Lord.

In the more ordinary course of daily life, a safety zone is first a place of comfort. For without comfort there is no recovery from the problems of life. But a safety zone must also go on to provide enablement and growth.

In my counseling office, for example, I see people who have had truly awful things happen to them: the loss of a child, a terminal illness, death, or divorce, to name a few. These people need comfort. But they also need to be able to go on. The comfort must be of the type that strengthens rather than weakens. A true safety zone provides refurbishment as well as comfort. It is not just a "comfort zone," as some call it. It is not self-indulgent. It is not an escape only. It is certainly not a permanent escape.

It is the nature of a safety zone to be a place of contrast. Where there is danger, it provides refuge. Where there is grief or loss, it provides comfort. Where there is confusion or fear, a safety zone provides enablement and strength. Often the vehicle for such a safety zone is provided within the context of acts of hospitality.

A while back I was reading *A Foreign Devil in China*, which relates the story of Ruth Bell Graham's family when they were missionaries in China. As I read, I was struck by the contrast between the harshness of the surroundings and the gentility of the hospitality within her parents' missionary home. The safety zone of hospitality was a vital factor in the family's coping with the brutality of the outside environment. Because their walk to school took them near a wall that was a favorite place for the Chinese to carry out their custom of throwing out dead babies, the Bell children were regularly exposed to death in its harshest form.

In an interview with Ruth Graham, after I referred to the horror of what I felt she must have experienced seeing those babies, she replied: "I think God brought me up tough for a good reason, and I'm grateful. It was tough training." Later in life, as the wife of the most famous evangelist of our time, she used that early training and "prayed early on for a tough hide and a tender heart."[4]

However, during her childhood in China, along with the "tough training," she experienced the softening influence of hospitality in her home. Sometimes it is the gentleness of this kind of safety zone that ensures that the abrasiveness of life around us doesn't break us, but makes us grow stronger.

In the book about Ruth Graham's family, Christmas 1929 is described as white with snow on the ground, the most white of all Christmases; dinner, replete with baked goose with chestnuts, English peas, creamed potatoes, homemade candy, and a host of other non-Chinese dishes; entertainment, ending with the singing of old Southern songs. This day provided a safety zone of hospitality for a group of people of all ages who might otherwise have felt lonely at that special time of year. It offered a temporary respite from the reality of life around them. It provided memories for future days when they would be separated from one another.[5]

Whatever else is involved in any given act of hospitality, it must always be designed to provide a respite from the impersonal world outside. It must be a parenthesis in the hurry of life. It must make one feel safe. It must nurture the stranger, or the friend, at the gate.

We all have places to which we retreat for comfort and refreshment when life gets rough. P. D. James's famous fictional detective Adam Dagliesh refers to "his own contrivances for keeping reality at bay." In *A Taste for Death,* he describes the safety zone of hospitality he observed in one British home, which brought back memories of his own.

> The tea was substantial. Thin crustless bread and butter, a plate of cucumber sandwiches, homemade scones with cream and jam, a fruitcake. It reminded him of childhood rectory teas, of visiting clergy and parish workers balancing their wide-brimmed cups in his mother's shabby but comfortable drawing room, of himself, carefully schooled, handing round plates. It was odd, he thought, that the sight of a coloured plate of thinly cut bread and butter could still evoke momentary but sharp pain of grief and nostalgia.

Watching Nellie as she carefully aligned the handles, he guessed that all their life was governed by small diurnal rituals: early morning tea, the cocoa or milk last thing at night, beds carefully turned down, nightdress and pajamas laid out. And now it was five-fifteen, the autumn day would soon be darkening into evening and this small, very English tea ceremony was designed to propitiate the afternoon furies. Order, routine, habit, imposed on a disorderly world.[6]

For at least one English home, this was the specific definition of the safety zone of hospitality. For others, in other homes and cultures, its focus might be different. Where formality might be the forte of one home, casualness or, more often, variety might be the focus of others. The food would certainly vary from culture to culture and home to home. But always there would be that quality of the open hearth, food and conviviality, nourishment and comfort, safety and joy.

MAKING YOUR HOME A SAFETY ZONE

The remembrance of a safety zone of hospitality is often evoked by one particular characteristic. Sometimes it's atmosphere: the fragrance of sweet peas blooming outside my aunt Lydia's door; the seemingly constant burning of wood in a large, stone fireplace; the smell of lavender in a guest room. Sometimes it's the comforting smell of food cooking or baking that becomes associated with a specific environment or event. With the help of modern-day conveniences, even those who work full time can come home at night to a house filled with the comforting smells of food: for example, cheese bread baking, on a timer, in the bread machine or mushroom chicken cooking all day in the slow cooker. Oddly enough, later in life, when we encounter that same food, it may suddenly seem very ordinary indeed. It tasted better when it was part of an important whole.

As children, a friend and I just adored malted milk tablets. We consumed jars of them. Then a few years ago I saw them advertised in a catalog. Enthusiastically I bought a bottle for each of us. The big moment came: we opened our bottles, and we each put a tablet into our mouth. For a brief moment nostalgia flooded over us. Then we looked at each other in horror. They tasted terrible. Neither of us has ever been able to figure out what happened, except that it was a different time and different circumstances.

Similarly, in my teens, late-Sunday-night theological discussions in the home of a young couple from my church were always accompanied by a large bowl of vanilla ice cream covered with sliced peaches. I looked forward each week to the *whole:* ice cream with peaches, combined with conversation—always at the same house, with the same people, in the same living room! Today peaches and ice cream are still tasty, but they are not as special to me as they were then.

Often, however, a certain food ritual developed early in life, and associated with a specific event, does remain, in the present, a special reminder of the sense of safety and comfort with which it was first associated. During my teens I attended monthly Bible studies taught in the home of a friend. The studies were always finished, as if by ritual, with tea served in various flowered porcelain cups and cookies served with napkins on which Scripture verses had been pasted. The tea, the silver teapot, the cups, and the napkins combined with the people and the house to make a *whole* that was eagerly anticipated. Tea still reminds me of refuge and refurbishment, and I still prefer to drink it out of porcelain cups.

The need for some kind of predictable community continues throughout life, and often the enjoyment of that community centers around some aspect of hospitality. Today I associate one of my friendships with homemade chili and the stories of my friend's Mexican heritage that go with it. My daughter makes such special apple pie that I have ceased to eat it anywhere but at her home! Her pie makes any occasion special. Blended with the smell of apples and cinnamon cooking in the oven, a simple meal, a conversation, or the recreation of watching a good movie together all become safety zones of sheer enjoyment.

Whenever I think of the vast variety in safety zones of hospitality, one recurring memory of childhood comes to mind: the wonderful smell of Swedish coffee cake baking early every Saturday morning, waking me up to that one free day of the week.

My mother always served her coffee cake with generous applications of butter and a cup of hot coffee. When life is sad as well as when it is happy, the British turn to tea and the Swedes turn to coffee. To the Swede, coffee can be both a comfort and a celebration; and, more often than not, when coffee is served in a Swedish home, coffee cake is nearby. The early-morning aroma of freshly brewed coffee and coffee cake baking in the oven, with its delicious scents of cardamom, cinnamon, and yeast, conveys a sense of hospitality and welcome, even in those who as children did not wake up to that delicious smell on Saturday mornings.

Beyond the comfort of coffee and tea and the rituals associated with them, other foods can provide respite in the middle of life's tensions. The idea of comfort foods, foods that in themselves evoke positive feelings, is viewed with dismay by those who would relegate *all* fat, sugar, and salt to the list of forbidden fruit. But many authorities on nutrition now admit that attempting total abstinence from foods we need to limit doesn't work. It just leads to bingeing and giving up even trying to cut down. What does work is *balance*. As a rule we need to limit our fat intake to 30 percent of our diet, and we need to distinguish between saturated and unsaturated fat. We also need to limit sugar and salt intake. *But* periodically we need to have our comfort foods as a sort of safety zone of recovery from the conflict of the world in which we live.

Some comfort foods are simply comforting in their texture or aroma or warmth, like bread pudding or chicken soup. Other comfort foods relate to our personal history, such as what our mother fed us when we were sick, or the dishes our grandmother always served on Christmas Eve. At times a dish reminds us of a person long gone, the way my aunt Esther's coconut cake or my mother's coffee cake do. Then the food comforts because it reminds us of that special person. Each of us has our unique memories: memories of taste, aroma, serving dishes, calendar dates, and very special people.

To cook someone's personal comfort food for him or her can be a special act of hospitality. Sometimes a woman will come into my counseling office full of rage because her husband has compared her cooking to his mother's. The wife is naturally hurt, and men need to be more sensitive to how such comparisons are generally interpreted. But wives need to remember that what the husband wants may have nothing to do with culinary skill, and everything to do with memories evoked by comfort foods from the past. Wise spouses will occasionally cook such foods for each other. (Men, too, can give such a gift of understanding to their wives.) ✐

Not what we give, but what we share,
For the gift without the giver is bare;
Who gives himself with his alms feeds three,
Himself, his hungering neighbor, and me.

JAMES RUSSELL LOWELL

✻ T·H·R·E·E

Given to Hospitality

A pastor of a small church is always meeting people for coffee. They go to coffee shops here and there; they meet in homes. More often than not, he and just one other person come together to talk. He does not require a group to justify his time. Moreover, while sometimes the people he meets with are from his church, frequently they are not. Some individuals come with heavy problems; others are just lonely. But many come to know Christ as their Savior, not only in that pastor's church after a fine sermon, but sometimes over a cup of hot coffee. Such is the potential for God to work through us in the safety zone of hospitality.

To be given to hospitality is a clear command to those who aspire to positions of leadership in the local church. Since sound biblical exegesis demands that we keep in mind that most early church leaders were men, then we must grapple with the fact that the command from God to be "given to hospitality" (1 Timothy 3:2 KJV) is most often directed toward men. Furthermore, these men were commanded to do more than just extend hospitality. They were ordered to "enjoy having guests in their homes" (Titus 1:8 LB), a standard that took the call to hospitality out of the realm of a mechanical fulfillment of duty and put it into the arena of God-given love for people.

Thus the Bible does not say, "If you are a man, you don't have to worry about hospitality." Rather, men are responsible for the existence of hospitality in their homes. They are to see to it that such hospitality occurs. Furthermore, presumably, they are to actively engage in the fulfillment of that command. After all, some of these church leaders were not married, so it cannot be automatically assumed that all acts of hospitality were to be handed over to wives. Perhaps the lesson to be learned is that men are not to consider themselves above the mundane tasks of washing dishes or grocery shopping. Nor should they underestimate their talents in food preparation or other creative skills that are involved in the giving of hospitality.

Many men have a culinary specialty all their own with which they entertain their friends. My father used to make his own pickled herring every Christmas. He would divide it up into glass jars and then give it to various people—from bank tellers to grocery clerks. On Christmas Eve, my father's pickled herring was a highlight of our Christmas feast. A male friend of mine was always known for his Saturday morning pancakes, which he made regularly until all of his children were grown and had left home.

Illustrating the use of another gift of hospitality is a young man I once knew who loved to clean up. Clean dishes sparkling in the china cabinet, dish towels neatly hung out to dry, a polished stove and a scoured sink: these made him feel good. Cleaning up was his contribution to hospitality, both at home and at church, where his gift was thankfully received by every cleanup committee. This young man did with joy that which he did best; for, indeed, the specific gifts of hospitality are to be developed and used with pride and pleasure.

For those, male or female, who feel that menial household tasks are too ordinary to be of value to the kingdom of God,

Amy Carmichael offers words that add perspective and balance. In her book *His Thoughts Said . . . His Father Said,* she has written of the importance of the seemingly unimportant:

> His thoughts said, My work is not important. Would it matter very much if a floor were left unswept or a room left untidied? Or if I forgot to put some flowers for a guest, or omitted some tiny unimportant courtesy?
>
> His Father said, Would it have mattered very much if a few people had been left without wine at a feast? But thy Lord turned water into wine for them.
>
> And the son remembered the words, *Jesus took a towel.*[1]

Truly no task of hospitality is too menial for any man or woman if it was not too menial for our Lord Himself. Furthermore, the capacity to offer hospitality in general is not limited to gender.

During one period in my life, one of the nicest times of hospitality that I experienced was on Christmas Day when I went to a friend's house for Christmas dinner—a dinner cooked by a man, at a man's house. The house was decorated with garlands of pine boughs. In the living room, near the large stone fireplace, stood a tall Christmas tree that extended to the top of the high, vaulted ceiling. Beneath it were piled colorfully wrapped packages. The aroma of a turkey roasting and a ham baking filled the house. Since my host had been a friend of mine since childhood, his guests included people I knew but might not encounter again for another year.

Christmas Day at my friend's house marked a highlight at the end of the Christmas season. For me it was a special end-of-the-year signpost, culminating the festivities marking the birth of our Lord Jesus Christ. It also introduced the week leading toward New Year's Day, which is a week of my own personal preparation for the new year ahead. Christmas Day at my friend's house was a safety zone.

A newer safety zone for my family has been a quiet Swedish Christmas at my home on Christmas Eve, followed by a buffet supper on Christmas Day when we meet with some close friends at a small airport restaurant. After the buffet supper, we go out on a patio by the runway of the airport, drink cappuccino, and exchange presents. Our major exchange of hospitality takes place on that large patio (I live in California!) where we listen to Christmas music, enjoy the lights, watch the planes landing and taking off, and share our holiday experiences with each other.

Then on New Year's Day a few friends, some different each year, come to dinner at my house where we enjoy the last of the Christmas decorations, exchange gifts, and commit the new year to the Lord.

All of these are times of hospitality that enable us to refurbish and go on. They have some level of predictability to them— familiar faces, holiday food, Christmas music, lights, Christmas trees and decorations, and enjoying people we care about and who care about us. That predictability makes them a safety zone.

SAFETY ZONES IN SCRIPTURE ✻

God is our ultimate safety zone. He is the only Being who never changes and never goes away. A verse of the old hymn "I Am His and He Is Mine" has always expressed so well for me this safety-zone quality of God:

> Things that once were wild alarms
> Cannot now disturb my rest:

Closed in everlasting arms,
Pillowed on the loving breast!
Oh to lie forever here,
Doubt and care and self resign,
While He whispers in my ear—
I am His and He is mine.

In God, we who are His children "have a place of refuge and security" (Proverbs 14:26). We have the only permanent safety zone this earth offers. And in a real sense God has invited His church, the body of Christ, to share this safety zone with others through the gift of hospitality.

It follows, therefore, that no gift of hospitality should be belittled. For "the eye can never say to the hand, 'I don't need you.' The head can't say to the feet, 'I don't need you'" (1 Corinthians 12:21). The most meaningful acts of hospitality do not require a palace setting or any other extravagance. In the Scriptures, most of the women—many of them widows—who are recorded as having entertained great men and prophets of God probably did not have huge ovens or large, convenient kitchens. And had they lived in our time, I'm sure they would not have waited until they had redecorated their kitchens, much less their houses, before they began to entertain. They simply shared what they had (as little as it often was), and what they had was more than enough.

An Old Testament story provides a remarkable example of the true nature of hospitality. One day while God's prophet Elisha was going about his daily business, he met a woman in a place called Shunem. The woman invited him for a meal. After that, Elisha made it a habit to eat at her house whenever he was nearby. This woman's home became a safety zone of provision and comfort for a man who traveled extensively and at times held precarious positions with the heads of government.

Later, the woman and her husband set aside for Elisha a room that contained simple furniture and a lamp. It was a *place*. It was a safety zone. And in this place he had a room that was uniquely his. It was always there for him. Knowing that must have given Elisha a sense of belonging when he was far away from home geographically (2 Kings 4:8–10). To provide a place, whether that place is concrete or whether it exists in the heart of a person who is always there for you: that is the essence of hospitality. Through such a place God Himself can minister.

Throughout the New Testament, too, we find definitive examples of the depth of hospitality expressed in simplicity. Paul wrote from prison to a fellow Christian, Philemon: "Please keep a guest room ready for me" (Philemon 22). He didn't say, "Could you put me up when I get out of here?" He asked for more. He needed a room to be kept ready, a place that would be there for him even when he was still in prison. It would be, as President Harry Truman once said, a foxhole in his mind. It would be a place of retreat, a safety zone in his mind until it could be an actual place of shared hospitality.

Paradoxically, while it stresses simplicity, the biblical standard of hospitality is a very high one. The emphasis is not on material goods but on the more costly giving of oneself. Proverbs 15:17 reads: "It is better to eat soup with someone you love than steak with someone you hate." Nineteenth-century American writer Ralph Waldo Emerson's definition of hospitality parallels the sense of the Scriptures: "Hospitality consists of a little fire, a little food, and an immense quiet."

Not only are we commanded to offer this kind of hospitality as a gift to those around us, but we are told that hospitality is an appropriate expression of enjoyment for all of us, even the one who gives the party. In the well-known story of the Prodigal Son, a father rejoices because his son who has wandered far away into a life of sin and ruin has returned. The immediate response of the father is "We must celebrate with a feast" (Luke 15:23). We must make merry. We must rejoice. Enjoyment is good for all of us. It provides a pause in the intensity of our task, adding a sense of lightness to a world bowed down with grief.

The feast for the Prodigal Son was an elaborate one. This is not an example of simple entertaining. The father provided appropriate clothing for his son and gave him a piece of jewelry; he brought out the fatted cow as the main course. Yet underlying all the elaborate and enjoyable festivities, the occasion provided a signpost that said: "This my son was dead, and is alive again; he was lost, and is found" (Luke 15:24 KJV). The other son was still favored: "Everything I have is yours," the father reminded him. But, he said, "It is right to celebrate" (Luke 15:31–32). It is right to mark out an important event with hospitality.

Who is to be on the guest list when we offer hospitality? Obviously, since enjoyment is one motivation, we will invite friends, family, those we like. But the Bible demands more. Entertaining for fun is just the beginning. When He saw the Pharisees fighting over who would be the most honored at a dinner party, Christ Himself said to the host: "When you put on a dinner . . . don't invite friends, brothers, relatives, and rich neighbors! For they will return the invitation. Instead, invite the poor, the crippled, the lame, and the blind. Then at the resurrection of the godly, God will reward you for inviting those who can't repay you" (Luke 14:12–14).

Christ is not telling us that we must stop entertaining people we like. To the contrary, attending *first* to the needs of one's own family is a biblical principle. What He is saying is don't offer hospitality with a jealous, competitive spirit or with the motivation of currying favor with the rich and powerful. Instead, we are to offer hospitality under His direction—the One who has become the Lord of our lives in this area of service as well as every other.

Proverbs 25:21–22 offers further instruction along these lines. "If your enemy is hungry, give him food! If he is thirsty, give him something to drink! This will make him feel ashamed of himself, and God will reward you."

With that sense of balance that so characterized his life, Charles Haddon Spurgeon, whom many consider to be the most outstanding preacher of nineteenth-century England, once said:

> Christianity was never intended to make men miserable. On the contrary, it has a tendency to make them happy. . . . Feasts of hospitality are good things. . . . The first house that we read of Christ's entering was "the house of feasting." He was at a marriage, at Cana in Galilee, and there he turned the water into wine. . . . It is well to entertain the sons of God; it is well to receive the wayfarer. This Christians ought to do more than they do now, and be "given to hospitality.". . . I will tell you the best dinner party that you can have. If you have "the blind, the halt, and the lame," and get them to sit around your table, you do more honor to your drawing-room than having a company of princes and nobles.[2]

Whether hospitality is extended to one's family or to other guests, at the core of good hospitality is how much you offer healing to the wounded spirit, encouragement along a difficult path, and hope where hope has long since disappeared. Food, atmosphere, and even material gifts of clothing and money are just useless tools until they are ignited by the love spoken of in 1 Corinthians 13:3, which declares: "If I gave everything I have to poor people . . . but didn't love others, it would be of no value whatever."

Such love must be of divine origin. In the little town of Le Chambon, that center of resistance during World War II, the work of rescue became overwhelming at times. At one point a woman came from another town to help. The newcomer first made her commitment on her knees in prayer to God to a task of hospitality that was to extend far beyond serving tea cakes and providing a place for afternoon chatter. She was to help in the actual saving of lives. For that she would have to give all. It would require divine love.

When she first arrived in Le Chambon, she asked to be called Jispa, a name she invented from the French phrase that means "the joy of serving in peace and in love." Extreme? Yes! But the specific task of hospitality to which she was called was also extreme. The name was important to her because she had a quick temper. The name was a sort of beeper, a personal alarm system. Long-term hospitality can be taxing, and hearing the name Jispa always reminded her not to give in to anger but to serve in love.

Hospitality is not always heavy. Sometimes it *will* consist of tea cakes and afternoon chatter. Sometimes it is offered just for fun. But it is always a gift that we offer to others. And in the deepest definition of the word *hospitality,* there is commitment and purpose. It is a work for God. ✻

Hospitality is a test for godliness because those who are selfish do not like strangers (especially needy ones) to intrude upon their private lives. They prefer their own friends who share their life-style. Only the humble have the necessary resources to give of themselves to those who could never give of themselves in return.

ERWIN W. LUTZER

🐿 F·O·U·R

The Gift of Hospitality

Coconut layer cake is what I immediately remember when I think of Aunt Esther. As I was growing up, "Aunt Esther's cake," as it came to be called in our family, was a highlight of most family functions. It was not the fanciest dessert that was served, for my mother was a gourmet cook and often made incredibly elaborate desserts. But for me, at least, any occasion worth celebrating was not complete without Aunt Esther's cake. It was a signpost that said: "This is an important occasion," and echoed the words of the little girl awed by the china and silver who said, "That means she loves us."

More remarkable still was Aunt Esther's special gift of hospitality in general. She and Uncle Blanton were never rich. They never even owned their own home. But wherever my aunt lived became a place of hospitality.

We did not have a television when I was growing up. TV was relatively new, and no one felt a particular need for it. On Saturday nights, however, shows like *I Love Lucy* and, later, *Gunsmoke* became favorites. For several years my family spent each Saturday evening at Aunt Esther's house. A part of the ritual was that Uncle Blanton and I would go downstairs to the basement, where the big freezer was. We would choose our favorite flavors of ice cream and then put several large scoops into each person's bowl.

Returning upstairs we would serve everyone and then settle down into comfortable overstuffed chairs to watch the evening's programs. (It was convenient that all of our favorite TV programs happened to be on Saturday night!)

Aunt Esther's Coconut Layer Cake • 156

Jell-O Cake • 162

Saturday nights became a safety zone of closeness that we looked forward to all week. TV, ice cream, a loving family, and a particular geographical place, my Aunt Esther's home, all combined to make a safety zone of hospitality. Uncle Blanton and I were very close. We were soul mates in our love of literature and theology. But it was Aunt Esther who knew how to make a home anywhere she went.

DISCOVER YOUR GIFT OF HOSPITALITY

No two places of hospitality are alike. Each is unique, with different foods, smells, fabrics, sounds, and forms of entertainment. Often the safety zone exists in a house or apartment. But it may also be a park bench, a restaurant, the woods, or the beach. When I was a child, the umbrella tree in our backyard was the place where we children would spread out a blanket, play with our dolls, and then have peanut butter sandwiches for lunch.

A place becomes a safety zone because of what people do with it. You don't have to have a big home, or a perfect kitchen, or a lot of money to provide a safety zone of hospitality. It is not what you have, but what you *do* with what you have that makes the difference.

Safety zones are as varied as the people who provide them. Some people are wonderful with strangers. Others are able to make the uncommunicative feel safe enough to talk. Still others have special talents in dealing with the very young or the very old. Some people have great creative skills and can devise unusual table settings, individualized gift wrappings, and elaborate cake decorations. A few have extra room in their houses and enjoy having overnight guests. Some have a talent for baking and may specialize in pies, cookies, or ethnic foods.

But whatever your particular talents may be—and you *do* have some—you need to recognize, cultivate, and utilize them. If you have a gift for conversation, don't spend all your time in the kitchen stirring soup. If you are skilled in making wonderful desserts, don't volunteer to bring salads to the church social. In the same way, your family may entertain large groups of people with ease and yet feel utterly overwhelmed by a dinner party for six. As one women said to me, "Large groups are so easy; they take care of themselves. It's small groups that scare me. Then I have to converse, and neither I nor my husband find conversation easy."

In addition to all of these human qualities, the glorious thing about being a Christian is that each of us is uniquely suited to provide a never-to-be-duplicated place of hospitality for those God brings to our hearth. The call to hospitality is a Christian call. And the unique task of hospitality, to which each of us has been called, is something to be discovered in much the same way that one chooses a life partner or a career. It is a divine calling. It is a divine command.

Hospitality can range all the way from offering a simple cup of cold water to giving a great, elaborate banquet. Christ extended hospitality when He fed the multitudes. Both Mary, who sat at Christ's feet, and Martha, who served, exercised their particular calling in hospitality. Jesus, Mary, and Martha each gave their distinctive gifts to others.

HOSPITABLE TO STRANGERS 🐚

While David was in the wilderness hiding from Saul, who was trying to kill him, David's presence was a "wall of protection" for the sheep who belonged to a man named Nabal and to those who tended them. Yet when David asked Nabal for food at the time of a special occasion, a request that was consistent with tradition at that time, he was abruptly refused. David was enraged and prepared to kill Nabal and his men.

One of Nabal's men who heard of David's plans went quickly and told Abigail, Nabal's wife. The man's closing comment gives insight into Nabal's character: "He's such a stubborn lout that no one can even talk to him!"

Abigail knew that obedience to God was greater than obedience to her husband. With swift presence of mind, she took bread, wine, meat, grain, raisin cakes, and fig cakes to David to try to appease him. Wisely Abigail appealed to David by referring to all that God was still going to do with his life: "When the Lord has done all the good things he promised you and has made you king of Israel, you won't want the conscience of a murderer who took the law into his own hands!" David's response was, "Thank God for your good sense!"

Within two weeks Nabal had died of a stroke, "for the Lord killed him." David's comment was, "God has paid back Nabal and kept me from doing it myself; he has received his punishment for his sin" (1 Samuel 25:1–39).

A simple act of hospitality was requested: a few cakes, some meat, some wine, some grain. It was requested by a man who was the only person in the Bible referred to as "a man after God's own heart"—a man whose descendants would include the future Messiah. Failure to meet that demand was punished by God.

Actually, David's reactions were consistent with the custom of that time, and even customs existing into the twentieth century. Commentators Jamieson, Fausset, and Brown explain: "The preparations of David to chastise his [Nabal's] insolent language and ungrateful requital are exactly what would be done in the present day by Arab chiefs, who protect the castle of the large and wealthy sheep-masters from the attacks of the marauding border tribes or wild beasts. Their protection creates a claim for some kind of tribute, in the shape of supplies of food and necessaries, which is usually given with great good-will and gratitude; but when withheld, is enforced as a right." However, "in making this vow utterly to destroy Nabal's house, David committed sin."[1] He went too far. Abigail's wisdom and quick action saved David from his own folly.

The incident illustrates in a striking manner that the call to hospitality is not to be taken lightly. It also emphasizes the broad meaning of the word *hospitality*. In Hebrews 13:2 we are commanded "to show kindness to strangers" (WEYMOUTH).[2] According to Strong, the meaning of the Greek word used here for hospitality includes the phrase *fond of guests* and the simple word *friendly*.[3]

I live in an apartment building that has a pool in the middle of the courtyard. The two-story building forms a horseshoe around the pool. One day two boys came off the street, sneaked up on the balcony, and prepared to jump over the pool deck into the water below. The jump is dangerous, but every summer at least two or three junior-high-age children give it a try. As these two boys balanced themselves, preparing to jump, a tenant shouted: "Don't you dare jump. You get out of here!" Most of them don't stop when they are shouted at. They just jump, swim, and run.

To my amazement the two boys stopped instantly and came downstairs. "Can we just swim across the pool once?" they asked politely. "No," the tenant said crossly. "You just get out of here."

These boys had obeyed where many would not, and letting them swim for a few minutes would have been a fitting reward—and might have encouraged future obedience. It would have been "friendly." It would have been a simple act of hospitality.

Hospitality can truly range from offering a cup of cold water all the way to giving a great, elaborate banquet. Christ extended hospitality when He fed the multitudes. Mary, who sat at Christ's feet, as well as Martha, who served, exercised their particular calling in hospitality. Each gave her own gift to others. What one does best is unique to each individual's gifts and calling.

ORGANIZATION: THE KEY TO HOSPITALITY

Once we discover and acknowledge our specific calling, the next thing we need to do is get organized. Organization is a major tool in carrying out hospitality.

Do any of you still remember the traditional model of organization that our parents and grandparents used to follow, before the days of modern conveniences and working mothers?

Wash on Monday
Iron on Tuesday
Mend on Wednesday
Churn on Thursday
Clean on Friday
Bake on Saturday
Rest on Sunday

While some of the tasks facing us today have changed from those of fifty or a hundred years ago, we still need to be organized if we're going to get things done.

Freezing food ahead of time, for example, can make the difference between effectiveness and chaos when you entertain. It also allows you to focus on your guests rather than on food preparation. If you make a casserole for dinner, make an extra one to freeze so that you can use it in an emergency. Some recipes actually make large enough portions for two small casseroles, like my recipes for chicken tortilla casserole and turkey meat loaf.

Chicken Tortilla Casserole • 193

Turkey Meat Loaf • 198

Bread and cookies can be frozen for relatively long periods of time and used in a variety of ways. For example, a special homemade bread can be instantly available to serve with soup for an unexpected guest. Cookies can be a treat for a child or an accompaniment with tea or coffee when someone drops by to chat. Likewise, a supply of frozen snack-like foods can be handy when you are faced with unexpected guests.

Years ago a friend introduced me to ham puffs: a tasty, nutritional hot snack that can be made ahead, placed in groups of six on a foil tray, and frozen. When a guest appears at the door, you can take one or more of these

Ham Puffs • 130

trays from the freezer, bake the ham puffs, and serve them within a few minutes. Offered with a beverage, they both refresh and help provide a relaxed atmosphere for conversation.

You can also freeze entire meals ahead of time. A good rule of thumb is to freeze several dishes ahead but leave the more perishable parts of the menu to be made closer to serving time, thereby minimizing how much there is to do when the guests arrive. For example, use a frozen casserole but make a tossed salad or cook a fresh vegetable.

Certain modern conveniences also allow for organizing ahead of time: bread machines, which can be set on a timer; slow cookers, which can cook a meal all day while the host or hostess is away from home; microwave ovens, which can reheat foods so that they remain oven-fresh in their taste and texture; and electric warming plates, which lengthen the time a buffet can stay on a table without endangering guests with food poisoning. These are just a few of the many time-savers available that, combined with some shrewd organization, can make hospitality easier and more effective at the same time.

Sometimes the gift of hospitality extends to inviting an overnight guest. If you find that having houseguests is the focus of your hospitality, your guest room should always be ready. Dust it regularly. Keep fresh sheets on the bed. Provide helpful items like pads of paper, pens, postcards and notepaper, books to read, some toilet articles, and fresh flowers to help make the room welcoming to your guest. Small travel-size items like bath gel, shampoo, mouthwash, disposable toothbrushes, hand lotion, and toothpaste arranged attractively in a small basket can provide practical help as well as a thoughtful touch. And even if you do not have the luxury of spare bedrooms, entertaining overnight guests is still a possibility with some organization.

When I was little, having overnight guests meant that we children gave up our bedroom until the guests left. Sleeping bags and the living room sofa provided temporary beds for us. The houseguests felt welcome because of the sacrifice and because of our obvious delight at having them in our home. We children, on the other hand, learned about giving up something for other people. We also had fun "camping out," as we called it. Having a couple of extra sleeping bags, quilts, and cots can be a part of the organization involved in effective hospitality in even the most simple of households. Recently I acquired a chair that opens up into a bed. It makes an extra room for a guest, and especially for my granddaughter. Last year, sleeping in the chair bed meant she went to sleep by the Christmas tree, which I then turned off once she was asleep.

SETTING LIMITS ✐

True hospitality is free. It is a gift that one person gives to another. True hospitality, however, should not tolerate abuse. Just because you cook well or have a big house does not mean that one person's whim becomes your command. It is important to declare boundaries regarding both how much you can do and what tasks God is calling you to. If you have houseguests, you may not want to donate a cake to the church on the same weekend. If your child is home sick, you may need to cancel a dinner party.

Furthermore, it is good to declare boundaries before those boundaries are crossed. Once a houseguest arrives, for example, it is hard to tell him or her to leave. But it is easy to say at the time the invitation is given: "We would love to have you stay with us until Monday," or "Why don't you spend two nights with us when you visit our town next month?" A specific time limit avoids confusion for the guest as well as for the host. Such limits also help prevent host or hostess burnout and create a more positive and relaxed atmosphere of welcome for the guest.

When you begin to dislike people in general or wish that you never had to cook another meal, it may be time for you to take a long pause. A fisherman cannot catch fish if his nets have holes. He cannot do his job. It is the same with burnout. We may have a call to an act of hospitality—a real call from God. But if we are burned out from meeting demands that were not from God, but which we accepted because we couldn't say no, then we will not be able to do those things God *is* calling us to do.

A need in itself does not constitute a call from God. If your child's second-grade class needs ten parents to make brownies, and they call you because they have only nine parents who are willing to help, that call—that need—does not require an automatic yes. Indeed, the needs that confront us will always be greater than our abilities to meet them. Unfortunately, in real life the needs are usually more serious than a need for brownies! And so it is even harder to say no. But the principle of *not* trying to do it all is an important one.

In reference to His own fatigue and that of His disciples, Christ said, "Let's get away from the crowds for a while and rest" (Mark 6:31). Spurgeon comments: "What? When the people are fainting? When they are like sheep without a shepherd? How can Jesus talk of rest? When the scribes and Pharisees, like wolves, are rending the flock, how can He take His followers on an excursion into a quiet resting place? . . . The Lord Jesus knows better. He will not exhaust the strength of His servants prematurely and quench the light of Israel. Rest time is not waste. It is economy to gather fresh strength. . . . Nor can the fisherman be always fishing; he must mend his nets. So even our vacation can be one of the duties laid upon us by the kingdom of God."[4]

Burnout is no more godly in the area of hospitality than it is in any other area of Christian ministry. Indeed, if you burn out, then you will be unable to extend hospitality to those whom God has called you to help uniquely. Often it is important to say no in one situation in order to say yes in another. It is important to know the call of God in each act of hospitality.

ANGEL UNAWARE ✍

A young man, Tim, stopped at the scene of a car accident a few minutes after it occurred. A seriously injured middle-aged woman lay in a pool of blood in the middle of the street. When Tim arrived she was unconscious.

Tim called for help. Then he stood alone, nervously waiting for help to arrive. The injured woman, who had been unconscious, began to revive and soon became hysterical. As she screamed and thrashed around, her bleeding increased. Tim stood, frozen with fear, watching as the woman seemed increasingly likely to bleed to death.

Suddenly, out of nowhere, a tall, middle-aged stranger in a gray suit came and stood beside Tim. "Go and pray with her," he said calmly.

Tim was a Christian, but the command—for it was a command—jolted him. He felt awkward walking over and praying. What if the woman didn't want him to pray? What if she got *more* hysterical?

"Pray with her," the stranger said again. And his demeanor did not invite debate.

"How does he know I'm a Christian?" Tim mumbled to himself. *Why doesn't he pray,* he thought. Then, giving the stranger a quick, hesitant look, Tim went over and prayed a short prayer with the woman.

The result was stunning. Immediately, she stopped screaming and thrashing around; and when the paramedics arrived, she had totally calmed down. Ultimately she did survive the accident.

After he had prayed, Tim turned to the stranger once again. But the man had vanished as quickly as he had arrived. The stranger was nowhere to be seen. As the sounds of the departing ambulance faded into the distance, Tim sat in his car and wondered about what had happened on this ordinary day that had suddenly become so extraordinary. Then, with a sense of awe, he started his car and drove away.

Because of the stranger's insistence, and in the most unlikely place, Tim had offered a basic gift of hospitality: the comfort and power of prayer with someone in desperate need. ✍

There was pleasure in eating strawberries, before they became quite common—in the first dish of peas, while they were yet dear—to have them for a nice supper, a treat. . . . It is the very little more that we allow ourselves beyond what the actual poor can get at, that makes what I call a treat—when two people living together, as we have done, now and then indulge themselves in a cheap luxury, which both like.

CHARLES LAMB

&∞ F·I·V·E

The Beauty of Simplicity

*B*y the way, thank you for helping me to entertain again," commented a young accountant as she turned to leave my counseling office.

Detaining her for a moment, I asked in honest confusion, "What do you mean?" Jo Ann and I had spent two counseling sessions together talking about her handling of coworkers. Entertaining was not a topic that I could remember discussing.

"You told me that I might entertain more if I didn't try to do it all so perfectly, if I emphasized one special dish and simplified the rest," she explained. "So I invited some friends for dinner and I tried a new approach. I made a rather complicated dessert that I've wanted to try for a long time. When I got to the tossed salad, however, I simply put in lettuce, tomatoes and cucumbers and left it at that. I resisted the urge to make each dish elaborate and perfect."

Then I remembered the end of our first session, when Jo Ann had explained that before she had gone back to working outside the home, she had been fond of cooking elaborate meals for both her family and guests. Often each recipe had represented hours of work. In her current job, however, her free hours had become so limited that she had stopped inviting guests for dinner.

Now once again she was able to extend hospitality, because she had begun to learn how to entertain without spending hours doing it. She had found ways to serve meals that were simple but attractive. In so doing, she had gained a sense of self-acceptance in sharing hospitality that allowed her to do less in the kitchen and find more enjoyment in her guests and in spiritual ministry to them.

There is a unique place in hospitality for elegance, gourmet cooking experiments, and an elaborateness that makes an occasion truly memorable, and we'll discuss some of those in the next chapter. But more frequently, simplicity is the key to success. Simplicity frees you to extend hospitality more easily and more often, so that it can become a true ministry of your Christian home regardless of other demands on your time and energy.

When I was in high school and college I attended a church that was truly given to hospitality. No visitor ever came to the church without being invited home for dinner by at least one family. The elders, in particular, took the ministry of hospitality upon themselves as part of their responsibility as the spiritual leaders in the church. Much nurturing and encouragement took place in homes over a meal or a late snack. And when it was needed an offer of lodging for the night was not unusual.

Besides being a successful businessman, one elder in the church was well-known for his Bible teaching, which influenced many people. While he and his wife had a lovely home and drove a Jaguar, no one seemed to be offended by these tokens of material success since the couple's lives were marked more by what they gave to others than what they themselves possessed. I still remember a Sunday afternoon I spent at their home.

Everyone took a short nap, and then there was an abundance of discussion on theological matters. As I recall, I was the only young person there that day, and so I felt special. As I was growing up it was from such conversations in a variety of homes, including my own, that I learned about writers like Amy Carmichael, Hudson Taylor, Harry Ironside, and C. A. Coates. I learned, too, about exercising discernment between writers who were biblical in their approach and those who were not; and my already well-developed inclination toward reading was further encouraged.

The particular Sunday afternoon that stands out in my memory was rounded out with a light supper of hot scones with ample servings of butter and jam, accompanied by hot tea, poured from a lovely silver teapot into hand-painted china cups. The supper could hardly have been simpler. But because the scones were freshly made and came to the table hot from the oven, and because of the beautiful tea service and the warm conversation, the meal was memorable.

On that Sunday afternoon over forty years ago, as we savored our scones and drank our tea, it was the combination that was significant: one special food, beautiful service pieces, stimulating conversation, and a sense of welcome. This is hospitality. Scones thrown together on paper plates on the kitchen table and eaten in haste would not have worked in the same way; the care with which the food was served was a vital factor in making each guest feel important.

Yet on a rainy night, in a kitchen filled with the smells of home cooking, a meal of hot, homemade soup, served casually in earthenware bowls and blended with good conversation could have been equally memorable. This, too, would have fulfilled the biblical command to be given to hospitality. Appropriateness in the choice of food and in how it is served, as well as a focus on those to whom the hospitality is being extended, are the key factors in the kind of hospitality that elevates the self-esteem of each recipient and bonds them together. Such hospitality creates what novelist Emily Brontë once referred to as the "hearth of home" feeling. It enables the guests to feel part of a whole for the time that they spend together. It provides memories for the future.

CREATING THE MOOD &

Care in serving does not need to take much extra time, and it does not always call for fine crystal and china. What it does require is a little thought and the development of a few simple creative skills. If the meal is to consist of simple foods, then ambience becomes even more important.

The use of match and contrast is always effective in serving. The old TV commercial where frozen dinners were served on crystal and fine china with lighted candles on the table, and no one could tell that the meal was not homemade, illustrates the point well. The simplest meal served with carefully chosen dishes, tablecloth, and decorative pieces will look like a feast. Conversely, the most elaborately cooked meal served poorly will neither impress anyone nor create an atmosphere of enjoyment.

It is often the simple but creative touches that give special meaning to a meal: cloth napkins tied with brightly colored ribbons, perhaps with a fresh flower tucked in the ribbon; inexpensive, bright blue water glasses that bring out an obscure trace of blue in the tablecloth; a thin slice of lemon placed in the water glass for flavor and color; ice cubes made from fruit juice or frozen with a mint leaf inside; candles and flowers on the table; a Bible verse printed on a card and placed by each individual plate.

Your table decorations can also express a theme or convey a message to your guests. Once, when I wanted to let a few friends know about the completion of a book that I was writing, I bought some tiny, white, clip-on bears with blue ribbons around their necks. I attached a small note to each bear that said: "It's finished!" Then I put one of the bears at each place setting. The overall effect was a simple but unique table setting. It was also a fun way to share an important event with a few close friends.

FAMILY MEALTIME

Special serving and decorating ideas don't have to be reserved for dinner guests. On any night of the week you can honor a family member by placing a card with a note of congratulations or even a small gift by his or her plate. This enables the entire family to applaud a special success or achievement. Such small acts of consideration are a vital antidote to feelings of isolation.

In contrast, family mealtime is too often a time when children are corrected and adults argue over issues that could be better handled elsewhere. In my counseling office I see many adults and children who dislike mealtimes because they are so filled with tension. Perhaps, in addition to our fast-paced living, a negative atmosphere is one reason so few families seem to eat meals together these days. To put it simply, people don't enjoy eating while they're being criticized or yelled at.

Mealtime should be seized as an opportunity for positive nurturing, both with good, nutritious food and with positive conversation. It provides a chance to express pleasure over a child's behavior or an adult's considerateness. It's a time to share experiences and discuss ideas.

As a child, I learned about my father's life as a boy in Stockholm when he would share those times over the evening meal. If we hadn't eaten together, I probably wouldn't know much about his boyhood, and I certainly wouldn't know as much as I do about my own roots. Dinner was also the time when I shared my own day's activities with my parents and sister and heard about the events of their day. Meals were one place where we got to know each other better as a family. They provided a safety zone of intimacy.

AVOID THE PERFECTIONISM TRAP ॐ

On one occasion, when I was invited to an informal, small luncheon at the home of someone known for her entertaining skills, from a culinary point of view it was a disaster. There were only four of us, and the invitation to stop for lunch had been a spur of the moment invitation as we were heading home from a meeting. Our hostess had bought the food at a deli, but it turned out to be, at worst, almost uneatable and, at best, certainly not fresh. She was mortified, but, after a simple explanation and apology, she did not dwell on the topic. We made do with a few basic items like bread and fruit and still came away refreshed from the experience. The attractive book-lined room, the fireplace, and the challenging conversation made the luncheon a memorable example of hospitality. It proved that sometimes so-called "failure" can succeed better than uptight "success." Brontë is right about the "hearth of home" feeling. Don't be so afraid of "failure" that you never try.

Important as hospitality is, its positive effects can be destroyed by perfectionism and an overemphasis on elaborateness. Focusing on one dish is an important way to simplify a meal. One Saturday afternoon, a friend and I went out to look at houses, just for fun. Joe had been in real estate years before, so his expertise made the adventure extra interesting. We were gone longer than

I expected, and as we came into my apartment, the aroma of chicken soup cooking in the slow cooker drifted out to us from the kitchen. Impulsively I exclaimed: "Why don't you stay for dinner?"

Enabling that impulsiveness was a pot of homemade soup that my friends and I laughingly call "stone soup," after the children's tale about soup made from stones and little else. For, in truth, stone soup is made from one or two chicken carcasses or half a turkey carcass—leftovers that most people throw away but which can be frozen and later made into soup.

Now as we came into the apartment the aroma was there and dinner was ready. We both exclaimed over how good the soup smelled. And I did not commit the cardinal sin of entertaining: *apologizing*. There is no reason to apologize for simplicity. Simplicity fosters the growth of intimacy. And intimacy, the ability to feel close to another human being, is a major tool in conquering loneliness.

Together, Joe and I found cheese and English muffins in the refrigerator, and we proceeded to make melted cheese sandwiches to eat along with the stone soup. It was getting dark outside, so I lit the candle that was already in the middle of my table. Everyday china, brightened by colored water glasses and colorful cloth napkins, which I usually have on hand, completed the relaxed feeling associated with the hearth. The scene was set for a nourishing meal and good conversation. My friend went home and tried his own pot of stone soup, and he's been making it ever since. He, too, has found that often one dish is enough, even for guests—especially when the invitation to share a meal is an impulsive one.

When the meal is not completely impromptu, a combined meat-vegetable entree can be made ahead of time and then served with a simple salad and bread. The combination of meat and vegetable simplifies the preparation of a meal. A main, make-ahead entree that I love to use is Chicken Divan. (This dish can be made several days ahead and frozen.) Once it is taken out of the oven, it can be placed on an attractive trivet on the table, in either a buffet setting or for a sit-down dinner, leaving guests to take portions as desired. Chicken Divan goes well with Fruit Delight salad, which can also be made ahead of time. This menu is ideal for the host or hostess who desires to serve a relatively special meal but still wants to be free from last-minute duties that keep him or her away from guests. Lance's Jambalaya also makes a lovely single-dish meal, accompanied by Fruit Delight salad or a tossed green salad.

Chicken Divan • 192

Fruit Delight • 200

Lance's Chicken Jambalaya • 194

Not only does a focus on one main dish contribute to spontaneity, it is also a great help to a family who is going to be away from home until dinnertime. It provides a workable solution to the problems of Sunday entertaining as well, when whoever cooks is often assigned the impossible task of cooking dinner at the same time he or she is at church!

In the small town of Necedah, Wisconsin, where my mother was born, my grandparents' home was the stopping place for visiting ministers. Often without prior notice, people came, ate meals, and even stayed several days in the big farmhouse. Indians, too, lingered nearby, and often they would come to my grandparents' house and trade their wares for food. Cousins and aunts and uncles who lived in nearby Chicago would come to visit their "country cousins" (as my mother and her family were sometimes called, to their utter disgust!). For my grandmother, planning meals and making sure that she had enough food on her shelves was a major priority.

Despite all the hard work of running a farm, however, my grandmother knew the importance of refinement in hospitality, even when that hospitality was just extended to her own family. She knew that *simple* was different from *tacky*. One of my favorite family pictures is of my mother as a little girl, all dressed up, having a picnic with her sisters on the bank of a creek. In the middle of the trees they sit demurely on the ground, a white tablecloth spread out before them, set with china cups and saucers.

PLANNING AHEAD

Considering the stress around us and the fast pace at which we all live, the safety zone of hospitality has rarely been more needed. But we also have much less time at home to prepare. For this reason, more than ever, planning ahead becomes a basic principle of entertaining.

One way I meet this challenge is by making as much use as possible of modern conveniences. The slow cooker is my most valuable tool when I need to come home to a cooked meal.

Mushroom Chicken • 196

Second only to the slow cooker for convenience (and that wonderful, home-baked aroma!) is the automatic bread maker. Like the slow cooker, using the bread machine creates a homey aroma throughout the house. With the use of a timer, that aroma can be planned for a specific time—like when you wake up, or at the start of a dinner party. These machines are not as expensive as they used to be; and considering that I now make all my own bread, I am saving in the long run. Also, I have the advantage of being able to add ingredients like bran, oats, soy flour, and dry milk, which contribute to the nutritional value—and the bread contains no artificial preservatives or additives. I have discovered, too, that if one is careful to balance dry ingredients with liquid, it is possible to alter recipes according to taste and even to create new recipes.

Cooking ahead of time, focusing on certain easy-to-make and/or easy-to-freeze recipes, and always having a good supply of certain adaptable and versatile foods on hand are the basic how-to's for the busy person who wants the freedom to spontaneously invite someone home for a meal.

It was four in the afternoon. I was just about to see my last patient of the day when the phone rang. Grabbing it quickly before I started the counseling session, I was surprised to hear the voice of John, a friend from out of town.

"Can we meet for dinner tonight?" he asked. "I'm still at the airport, but I can be there by seven."

Quickly I calculated in my mind: What did I have in the way of food? Could I even think about having dinner at seven, when I only finished work a little after six? This time I was lucky. My house was in good order, and I had the right ingredients on hand.

"Let's have dinner at my place," I found myself saying. "I'll be through in an hour."

With less than an hour left once I finished work, I would need help. I called a friend who lived nearby and had a key to my apartment, since she walked my dog, and asked her to go to my apartment and take out two steaks, a package of frozen raspberries, and two frozen potato boats to defrost. She also helped me out by putting out fresh towels in the guest bathroom and setting the table with everyday china and cloth napkins, enclosed in colorful wooden napkin holders with little carved figures on them.

When I got home, I spent ten minutes putting together a dessert I call Berry Swirl: alternating layers of vanilla ice cream, defrosted frozen raspberries, and whipped cream in parfait glasses, topped with additional whipped cream and a raspberry. Once the glasses are filled I put them into the freezer. Then about twenty minutes before dessert time I take them out and leave them in the kitchen until time to serve them. This way the layers soften and trickle down into each other, giving the effect of a fancy, hard-to-make mousse.

I once had an embarrassing experience with this dessert. I had served a dinner of homemade bread and stuffed chicken. My simple dish was Berry Swirl. One of my guests who is an excellent cook—and always makes a success out of complicated recipes—tasted the dessert and exclaimed: "This is a wonderful mousse. Would you mind giving me the recipe?" For one terrible moment I panicked: How was I going to explain ice cream, frozen raspberries, and whipped cream to *her*? How would I tell her it wasn't a mousse? Then, just when I decided it didn't matter and I would tell her the truth, the subject changed and she forgot to ask me again!

On the night of my dinner with John, I remembered the incident with amusement as I put the parfait glasses into the freezer. Then I took out lettuce, tomatoes, and a few radishes to make a simple tossed salad. I put a few bread sticks into a bread basket, put the potato boats into the oven to bake, and placed a candle on the table. (I could have made Rice Pilaf if I'd had more time,

Potato Casserole • 150

Rice Pilaf • 190

but the potato casserole was already in the freezer and therefore easier and quicker to use.) Essentially dinner was ready, with ten minutes to spare. I took the extra ten minutes to sauté a can of sliced mushrooms to serve with the steaks, which could be broiled after John arrived.

My last-minute dinner had two relatively special dishes: Potato Casserole and Berry Swirl. These, along with the sautéed mushrooms, offset the simplicity of the broiled steaks.

Dinner that night looked good and tasted even better. John couldn't figure out how I'd done it. And on many days I simply couldn't have. But on those days, a quick sandwich and soup would work just as well—as long as they were enjoyed in the safety zone of hospitality. But with the help of a well-stocked shelf and freezer and some ongoing planning, sometimes a rather elaborate meal can be served on relatively short notice. For example, I like to buy a large cut of top sirloin when it is on sale and have it cut into small steaks, which I then freeze. In that way I always have steaks available for an emergency. Cans of mushrooms and mushroom soup; fried noodles, bacon bits, or croutons to top a

Molasses Sticks • 174

Nut Brittle • 147

tossed salad; frozen vegetables and plenty of lettuce and tomatoes; ginger ale or fruit juice to serve with Ham Puffs before the meal: these are a few of the things that I like to have on hand, ready to use. It is also handy to have some type of sweet snacks in the pantry. I like to use Molasses Sticks or Nut Brittle, but each household's needs will vary.

What was important about my dinner with John was that most of the work was done before he arrived. For one hour, life was a little hectic. But by the time my guest arrived, I could relax and focus on our conversation, not on food preparation. For both of us, the quietness of my home and the sustenance of good food provided a safety zone of hospitality that felt good after a long, busy day.

As a tape of the London Philharmonic Choir singing "Amazing Grace" played in the background, I thought that even the angels might feel the sense of peace in this place in the middle of a world that is never at peace. And once again I thought of the words of C. S. Lewis: "Christ who said to the disciples, 'Ye have not chosen me, but I have chosen you,' can truly say to every group of Christian friends, 'You have not chosen one another, but I have chosen you for one another.'"[1] Such friendship is nurtured in the hearth of home. ❧

To love is to give one's time. We never give the impression that we care when we are in a hurry. To exercise a spiritual ministry means to take time. If we want to save our time for more important matters than a soul, we are but tradesmen.

PAUL TOURNIER

A Touch of Elegance

large, carved mahogany table spread with a white linen tablecloth and neatly folded cloth napkins; shiny silver cutlery; sparkling, clear crystal glasses and white glistening china at each place setting; the accent of a gold-etched sugar and creamer; a large, clear crystal bowl filled with multicolored roses, fresh from our garden: this is my childhood memory of *special*. A soft breeze from the garden, combined with the scents of freshly cut roses and lemony furniture polish completed the scene.

Family visitors from out of town, a birthday, and, on a less elaborate level but definitely more formal than on other days, Sunday dinner: such were the occasions for formal entertaining. But *formal* never meant stuffy or boring. It meant dress-up clothes, good food, and stimulating conversation. Such occasions were infrequent and therefore eagerly anticipated. They were *special*.

Because of its contrast to more ordinary times of hospitality and because of the effort expended in providing it for a guest, elegance stands out. It becomes another signpost—a signpost that says, "You are important to me" or "This event we are celebrating has significance" or "Welcome!" or "Farewell!" or "You have our support."

The stepsister of Anne Frank writes of the significance of just such a signpost. Somehow, she and her mother survived Auschwitz, one of Hitler's notorious death camps. Their degradation and suffering there had been unspeakable. At a peak of despair, the young girl had watched as an SS woman had filled her precious food mug with human waste and then thrown its contents all over her skirt and legs. And there would be no shower allowed until the end of the week!

When they were at last free from that terrible place and on a ship of repatriation, the mother and daughter were given beds with mattresses, clean white sheets, and blankets. Making themselves look as good as possible under the conditions from which they had emerged, the two went to the dining room for dinner. Says the daughter:

> As we walked through the doors to the restaurant, we saw that every table was laid with a spotless white tablecloth, silver-plated cutlery, shining china and sparkling glasses. It took my breath away. Only a few weeks ago we had been drinking from chipped tin mugs. Mutti burst into tears as she took it in. We were really very touched by the way we were being treated as human beings again.[1]

As the food was served the former inmates ate voraciously. Food was what they needed. They could not eat silver, china, and crystal. But it was that first look at incredible elegance that began reversing the dehumanization process to which they had been subjected for so long. It was that touch of elegance that made them feel once again like human beings.

Special times of hospitality are destroyed by ostentation, competitiveness, perfectionism, and stiff manners. But *true* elegance makes an occasion memorable and increases the sense of self-worth of the people receiving the hospitality. Fake elegance says: "Watch how well I entertain," or "Look at how many expensive and rare things I possess." True elegance says *"You* are *special,"* and forgets itself.

When I was a child, shopping malls did not exist; at least they didn't exist anywhere near where we lived. Shopping for clothes, therefore, always necessitated a trip downtown. Buying clothes for school in the fall was a yearly ritual, a ritual that became one of the safety zones of my childhood. Shopping at Christmas was another ritual, different in focus, but equal in the delight it provided. For each of these shopping rituals, my mother and I always dressed up in our Sunday best and took the streetcar near our home. As a child I eagerly anticipated the ride on the streetcar, which culminated in a dark, long, delightfully scary tunnel that ended the trip with a proper flair. Within a short walking distance from the streetcar station were all the stores.

On our walk from the station, we sometimes looked at puppies in the pet store and watched gimmicky windup toys that were sold by the occasional street vendor. And while we were at the two or three big department stores where we picked out my school clothes or our Christmas gifts, my mother always gave me time to look at books and choose at least one to buy and take home.

The real highlight of the day, though, was lunch in a fancy tearoom, a place where children were rarely taken. One tearoom that I remember in particular was located in one of the department stores. It was on the mezzanine, on a half-circle overlooking the floor below, and overhead were huge, sparkling crystal chandeliers. The china and silver were fancy; the food was delicious and dainty. But my memory of that place always focuses on those sparkling chandeliers.

Despite the elegance, the atmosphere was relaxed. The waitress usually gave me special attention, and my mother and I talked about school or about what clothes I had gotten or would still get. It was a rare time of uninterrupted intimacy and conversation, just between my mother and me. And for me, the chandeliers added the final touch of elegance that made those lunches unforgettable. Because of the elaborateness of the scene, I felt grown-up in a grown-up world—and very special.

Elegance says "You are special" or "This occasion is special" or, in the example of the chandeliers, "For this moment, at least, you are grown-up." Elegance makes a time of hospitality memorable and causes a guest to take seriously the reason for the hospitality.

WHEN TO USE ELEGANCE

To determine the specific mixture of formality and casualness that is appropriate, first ask yourself, "What is the purpose of this particular act of hospitality?" If you want to honor someone's achievement, use the formal atmosphere as a signpost of something out of the ordinary. If you want serious discussion to ensue, create a formal but comfortable mixture of elegant and simple. If you want total relaxation, serve hot dogs outside on paper plates! A second question to consider is, "To whom is this hospitality being extended?" For example, if the guest list consists of people who are ill at ease socially, focus on simplicity.

Touches of elegance can be expressed in the physical atmosphere of a place, in the table setting, in the choice of foods served, by the type of background music, by the clothes worn by the host or hostess, and even by the manner in which the invitation is given. Usually, elegance is expressed in a combination of these ways. For most entertaining, perhaps it is still best to mix elegance with simplicity: for example, sending a written invitation for a small party. That way the elegance is not overwhelming. Besides, most things show up best by contrast.

As a practical footnote, it is good to remember that formality can also subdue people! All of us encounter individuals who don't know where to stop. They joke around too much. Or they simply take over. Yet we care about them and don't want to completely drop them as friends. People tend to behave in a way that is consistent with the way they are dressed and the atmosphere in which they find themselves. I've always said that when the public school where I used to teach dropped its dress code, student behavior immediately became more uncontrollable. The barriers were down.

The same principle applies to hospitality. Boundaries need to be established, and some of those boundaries can be automatically stated in the formality of a situation. What is important to keep in mind is that you are the host or hostess. *You* set the mood by the way you plan an event. *You* establish how long the houseguest stays and what kind of entertainment is provided at a dinner party.

MIXING ELEGANCE AND SIMPLICITY

Obviously, however, the purpose of elegance and formality in entertaining goes well beyond the more negative aspect of setting boundaries. Often in my entertaining I mix people whom I hope will influence each other or whom I simply want to introduce to each other. For such times I find that a setting with a sharp contrast between formal and informal can be effective. Bright colors, casually arranged flowers, music that provides warmth and inspiration, and candy favors at each place provide the casual touch. For contrast, cloth napkins, good china, silver, and crystal, and at least one impressive food dish, encourage relaxation combined with serious intent. Two dishes I like to serve for this type of event are Princess Charlotte Pudding and Monkey Bread.

This bread is elaborate, yet casual in the sense that it is eaten more communally. "Enjoyable Serious" could describe the desired effect!

Mixing formal and casual can be very effective in helping to create the atmosphere of the open hearth. My good china, for example, has an elaborate green and white pattern. I rarely use this china exclusively, because by itself it looks too ornate. Mixing my china with some white serving bowls or a piece of gold-painted porcelain creates a setting that is much more relaxed and attractive. Don't be afraid to mix, match, and contrast. Fresh flowers, cloth napkins tied with bright ribbons, bright-colored candles, and an occasional shell or two placed near the candlesticks all tend to soften the effect, keeping formality from becoming stiff and uncomfortable.

In the same way that you need to organize a dinner party to fulfill your desired goal, you also need to keep specific goals in mind in furnishing your house or apartment. In choosing and furnishing your home, you set the mood for future entertaining. I prefer an eclectic approach myself: a Chinese chest that reminds me of my aunt Ruth's work in China, several carved mahogany pieces from the family, an old trunk covered with gold leaf and loved more for its uniqueness than its value. Meaningful objects, plenty of photographs, some plants, a canary in a cage, and a few sharp contrasts in color provide a backdrop against which I can best function in a ministry to others and in just enjoying my friends.

Hospitality is an area where you can exercise your own creativity and personality. Do what works *for you*. But remember, in furnishing your home you are laying the groundwork for what God can do through you in that *place*. These decisions are important and need to be made prayerfully. A fundamental question might be, "Is this an atmosphere in which the Lord Jesus Himself would be comfortable?" Ostentation or sloppiness, crude artwork, or a home that is characterized by keeping up with the proverbial Joneses does not honor the one whom, as Christians, we have established as the Head of our home.

Through the years I have observed, in many settings, that mixing the casual with the formal, the simple with the elegant provides the most comfortable setting for hospitality.

In the choice of foods the same principle applies. For the sanity of the host or hostess, as well as the waistlines and digestive systems of the guests, balance a couple elaborate dishes with something more simple. Try serving one or two elaborate dishes (such as Cheese Straws) with a simple green salad. If you're having soup, accompany it with a dessert-like salad (such as Betty's Dessert Salad) or a fancy dessert (such as Kisses, Boston Cream Cake, or Lemon Fluff Pie). A plain roast goes well with the more elaborate Monkey Bread (see index) or a simple Yorkshire pudding. Sometimes even a vegetable dish can be elegant, like my recipe for Vegetable Terrine. This dish has a twofold benefit: you

Cheese Straws • 129

Betty's Dessert Salad • 200

Kisses • 152

Boston Cream Cake • 157

Lemon Fluff Pie • 178

can serve it hot or cold, and it actually tastes better if prepared the day before.

Round out a meal with a simple salad, or with a relish plate of olives, celery, and carrot sticks, along with something a little more fancy, like canned miniature corncobs or small sweet pickles. Salsa and guacamole are two other versatile items that can be used either as an hors d'oeuvre or as a part of the meal.

The more elaborate the decoration or the food, the greater the need for simplicity to offset it. Steamed vegetables served with a main dish that is higher in fat content; gold serving pieces or a variety of bright colors on a background of white; a light entree served with a rich dessert: all these will create the most dramatic effect and save a dinner party from appearing overdone and tasteless. And any meal can benefit from small but special touches like sprigs of parsley on the plates, mint leaves in a cool drink, lemon slices in the water glass, fresh flowers, and candles.

Try serving after-dinner coffee with one of the flavored dairy creamers now available; use small chocolate bits in place of sugar; or offer whipped cream or chocolate-flavored whipped cream in place of the usual cream. Any of these will transform a cup of coffee into something special; and the process of choosing what to put into the coffee provides an additional opportunity for relaxing conversation. Also, serving a special after-dinner coffee means you can pull out that rare single piece of china or crystal or that silver tray that up to now has sat unused in the cupboard.

Sometimes it is effective to serve elaborate food casually in a buffet. Recently I served a birthday brunch that consisted of a breakfast casserole, a variety of homemade muffins, a loaf of lemon bread, and fruit—buffet style. Then for dessert I served a Nut Torte, which was particularly elegant, but could be made ahead of time. It was a hot summer day, and so the emphasis was on cool. Cool berry

Nut Torte • 164

drinks with lots of ice, a color scheme of pale yellow and green, and casual dress made the day thoroughly enjoyable. Yet the formality of the table setting and the foods served said: "Please be comfortable and relaxed; but know that this is still a special occasion."

For those who occasionally invite guests for breakfast, or even for one's own family breakfast at home on the morning after a major dinner (like Christmas or New Year's), my daughter Rayne has developed a wonderful muffin-puff type recipe that is nourishing and goes well with fresh fruit.

Under the fast-paced pressure that confronts all of us, it is sometimes better to have friends over for dessert than to wait until "there is time" to have them for dinner and then never do it. Sometimes, too, particularly when you want to invite a larger group, or where the act of hospitality is geared toward introducing

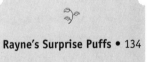

Rayne's Surprise Puffs • 134

new people to each other, a shorter time of dessert and coffee may be more enjoyable for everyone involved. If the group is small, this may be a good time to make a well-tested but more complicated dessert. Dishes of nuts and candy, or even cheese crackers, placed strategically around the house will add to the feeling of warmth and welcome.

For a small group, invited with the goal of meaningful conversation, a light supper and/or dessert around a fondue set can be very enjoyable. And don't forget, a fondue set can be used in a variety of ways, ranging from chocolate fondue as a dip for pound cake and pieces of fruit, to melted cheese and French bread, to a full meal of vegetables and meat. A fondue meal becomes an intimate sharing experience, so be sure that the people involved are compatible.

TRUE ELEGANCE

C. S. Lewis was fond of saying that there are no ordinary people. Every person we ever encounter is utterly irreplaceable. There will never be another you. There will never be another me. More important than that, you and I are immortal souls made in the image of God Himself. Viewed from this vantage point, hospitality extended to another immortal being is awesome indeed, so don't be afraid of elegance.

Elegance is not glitz. Elegance is something that makes our encounters with other immortal souls unforgettable. The time and effort that we put into such occasions become our gift to these unique beings who, like us, are made in the image of God.

Several years ago, I wrote a book about a difficult subject. After it was published, my daughter and a close friend planned a celebration: a very special dinner. The invitations were handwritten but formal and were sealed with a gold shell. The guests were seated at several small tables, each covered with a lace tablecloth and set with the finest china and crystal and decorated with fresh flowers. At the main table was a bowl of white roses to symbolize one of the topics of the book: the Resistance Movement during World War II.

The meal itself consisted of a complicated chicken dish, which took hours of preparation, and Betty's Dessert Salad (see index). Dessert was ice cream, in a variety of flavors, sculptured into pieces of fruit, arranged in a single basket so that it looked like an actual basket of fruit, and served with cookies. (This gorgeous ice cream fruit basket was prepared by a remarkable ice cream shop. The ice cream was well frozen, with a liner in the basket, and packed in dry ice until served.)

Other miscellaneous items that said "this is special!" were a dish of almond candies covered with a thin, edible silver coating; a small, hand-painted picture of a lighthouse, symbolic of the message of the book and given as a gift to each guest; and small, individual boxes of chocolates to take home.

Admittedly, this was not just a touch of elegance. This *was* elegance! But it was also a time that provided lifelong memories. Furthermore, it was accomplished in a small kitchen in an apartment.

At the end of the evening we remembered the Lord in the taking of Communion. As the bread was passed, and then the cup of wine, we were a small body of believers, but part of that larger body, worshiping God for what He had done and for who He is. It was an elegant evening climaxed by a simple worship service.

As I work at my computer, I can look across my desk and see the small picture of a lighthouse from that book party, and I recall that elegant evening. Yet paradoxically, the part I remember most of all is that simple, but profound, ending. ❧

It was the policy of the good old gentleman to make his children feel that home was the happiest place in the world; and I value this delicious home-feeling as one of the choicest gifts a parent could bestow.

WASHINGTON IRVING

❧ S·E·V·E·N

Entertaining Children

"Not leftovers again," groaned Justin as his mother took a bowl of spaghetti out of the refrigerator for dinner.

"It's perfectly good food, and you'll eat it," responded his mother.

The scene was a common one. Both Justin and his sister, Katie, hated leftovers—even leftover food they had liked when it was fresh.

The creative mother in this case decided to change her tactics. Rather than throw away good food or continue listening to the complaints of her family, she decided it was all a matter of how leftovers were presented.

Leftovers were not called *leftovers* anymore. They were served buffet style and were now labeled *smorgasbord*. The table was set for a sit-down meal, sometimes made even more special by candlelight. Thus the setting itself implied the opposite of leftover.

She would reheat and serve a piece of chicken, a serving of spaghetti, a portion of casserole, and some slices of pot roast with a fresh green salad or a favorite vegetable dish. Then each member of the family could choose his or her main entree from the available foods, along with a helping of salad or vegetable. If spaghetti turned out to be the favorite dish of too many people, then whoever got the spaghetti was now considered lucky rather than just a victim of leftover food. Leftovers became special.

Leftover Night became Smorgasbord Night. It was all in the presentation.

Smorgasbord Night became instructive, too. The children learned that food is not something to be wasted and that the same dish can be served twice and still taste good. They learned to share. Usually there was not enough of any one dish for everyone to have it. So Smorgasbord Night provided the perfect opportunity for the parents to encourage sharing and giving up something one wants because another person wants it, too. The children also learned the art of taking something plain, like leftover food, and making it into something very tasty. They learned to make do with what they had rather than always having to have something new and sensational, even in a food. Above all, they learned the importance of family and love and candlelight.

WHY HOSPITALITY FOR CHILDREN?

Hospitality for children should provide fun, but it can often be an effective tool for nurturing as well. One little girl was allowed to choose the menu for her birthday dinner. Being only six, nutrition was not high on her list! She chose chocolate milk, chocolate cake, chocolate ice cream, potato chips, and spaghetti. The only adult interference came when her mother offered to make a nutritious salad, a suggestion that was urged upon the child "because your grandparents are coming!" The dinner was served on the family's best china and crystal, and the little girl felt like a princess. It was *her* day, her birthday. And, in reality, the dinner was no worse nutritionally than all the junk handed out at Christmas or Easter.

At sixteen, this young woman still regales her friends with stories of that special birthday when the adult world bent its wisdom to the desires of childhood fantasy. She learned something, too, from this act of hospitality. She learned that if you're going to serve junk food as the occasional exception to good nutrition, provide at least one healthy dish to go with it. In fact, even at that fairly young age she began to understand the difference between junk food and healthy food, thanks to that birthday. When her mother urged her to add a salad because the adult guests would enjoy it, the girl also learned something about selflessness and sharing.

Even in celebrating a major event, like a birthday, it is not necessary to provide a whole meal in order to extend hospitality to a child. A Candle Cake served to each guest, with its singular candle in the center of what looks like a small, white snowball, will make a birthday memorable. Every child, whether the birthday child or a guest, enjoys having his or her very own special cake. For an outdoor celebration in the backyard or in a park, where a general mess will not be a problem, try

Candle Cakes • 159

Ice Cream Cake Cones • 161

serving individual Ice Cream Cake Cones. Because you do this outside, spilled sprinkles and tipped-over cones will not dampen the spirits of an otherwise fun time.

Any individual treatment at a celebration of a birthday, graduation, the end of a school term, or the winning of a baseball game makes a child feel special. A plate used only for serving birthday cake to the birthday person adds a simple individual touch for that occasion. Some people have a cake holder that plays "Happy Birthday." When my mother was a child, my grandmother had cups and saucers that she brought out only for special occasions. The use of these dishes said to the person being honored: "You are special."

It is important, however, not to feel that each thing that is done for one child has to be done at the same time in the same way for another child. Keep your overall treatment of children fair and equal. But just because one child has a big birthday party in the park doesn't mean that Candle Cakes at home or a trip to the zoo for another child isn't fair. Similarly, a small celebration one year after a larger one the year before may be appropriate. Sometimes the concept of overall fairness has to be explained to children when they begin to compare too much. Otherwise you (and they!) will be counting the number of items in each child's Christmas stocking, regardless of the variation in the value of the items. When they grow up, the pattern will be there. If you loan Fred a hundred dollars, you will feel you have to loan the same amount to Sue and Bob and Sally, even if they don't need it!

One of the most important results of hospitality to children is the development of a better self-image. Extending hospitality to your children or to their friends means you take them seriously as human beings. Much more important than all the creative ideas is the adult interaction with the children. Children need to be heard and conversed with, and hospitality provides a place for conversation. Many a conversation that has shaped a child's thinking for life has occurred over a simple plate of cookies and a glass of cold milk. Never forcing, but always allowing a child to tell you how he or she feels is a great gift to give a child.

Elaborateness and money cannot buy such opportunities. Simplicity combined with love and time can be of far greater value than things. Not long ago someone told me about an event she had attended, where a small boy and girl were given the most opulent, extravagant, and terrible birthday party a child could have. All kinds of people came to this party—friends and acquaintances of the parents, but people the children didn't even know. While the adults sat and drank in one room, the two children and a few of their friends stayed in another room and opened some thirty gifts each. The gifts were expensive, to the point where any one of the gifts would have been enough for an entire birthday. After opening thirty gifts, the children were tired, bored, and indifferent to what they had received. Neither parent was unselfish enough to sit and watch their children open even one gift; and without the gift of love everything else was empty. Even after their so-called birthday party was over, their parents were nowhere to be found: a nanny put the children to bed while the parents slept off the effects of their own celebration.

In contrast, celebrations and the sharing of certain foods can build and nurture the closeness of traditions in a family. And traditions provide a safety zone of comfort and refreshment for everyone concerned.

Certain traditions, such as birthdays and Christmas, provide obvious opportunities for comfort, nurturing, and just plain fun. But there are less obvious traditions that many of us valued as children and carried into adulthood. One child's grandmother had a tradition of taking her to lunch at a cafeteria they both enjoyed, and then they would go to a movie. A young father took his small son out for a hot fudge sundae when the child's grades came up dramatically, a reward the child enjoyed and profited from more than the usual gift of money. A school administrator, who often came home late from meetings during the week, made pancakes for his family on Saturday morning from his own special recipe. With repetition, all of these became traditions.

When I was little, my mother always made Swedish pancakes when guests dropped by for Sunday night supper or for a late, leisurely family breakfast. They were thin and buttery, and to eat them one spread them with butter and syrup or jam and then rolled them up like crepes. They were always served with plenty of bacon. When I spent the night with our next-door neighbors, usually on a Friday night, they always made German pancakes, or Eierkuchen, the next morning. These pancakes were small and thicker than Swedish pancakes, and they were served with homemade syrup and freshly squeezed tangerine juice from the fruit grown on the trees in the neighbors' backyard. These unplanned rituals and traditions became a safety zone.

HOSPITALITY AS A TEACHER

Added to the nurturing of self-image and the building of traditions, hospitality offered to children inevitably fosters the development of values. In my family, my parents stressed the attitude that our cup was always half-full rather than half-empty, and they illustrated this in the way they extended hospitality. Rainy days were a good, if simple, example. Rainy days were always wonderful days. When I was very small they meant a new book of paper dolls or a fresh box of crayons, usually bought with great delight as my mother and I, bundled up in our raincoats and rain boots, made a foray to Woolworth's. (For younger readers, Woolworth's was a chain of "five and dime" stores, combining all the delight of a toy store and a department store—on a small scale.)

After I started school, I always knew that when I came home in the rain I would find my mother baking cookies or making a special dinner. Our childhood favorites were Tuna Roll or Pork Sausage Casserole, served with Tomato Aspic salad. With the aroma of good food in the house, and the good spirits that went with it, it was impossible to feel gloomy just because it was rainy and dark outside. In fact, the gloom outside just emphasized the happiness within! Rainy weather became a fun time. And, more important, as a family we learned how to make bad times good.

Tuna Roll • 197

Pork Sausage Casserole • 149

Tomato Aspic • 203

The lessons learned in childhood have remained. After my mother's death, a friend came over to make dinner. Though I hadn't had Pork Sausage Casserole in years, I found the recipe and my friend made it. After all those years, the taste and memories of this comfort food still provided a safety zone. I had learned of comfort from my mother years before, and that held me in good stead, even after she had gone to be with the Lord.

To this day, I love rainy weather, and I have an inner instinct that compels me to try to make good times out of bad ones. When I had surgery a while back, I actually looked forward to at least being close to the sea for a few days. True, I would have given a great deal to not have to face the surgery, but my focus tended to go toward that time of refurbishment *after* the surgery was over and the meaning I could derive from it, rather than the surgery itself.

Perhaps my way of dealing with illness goes back to those childhood days as well. When I was a child, polio was feared to the point where we were at times forced to avoid public places. Penicillin wasn't in common use until late in my childhood, and even ordinary illnesses were treated with great seriousness. Yet the impact of my childhood illnesses was lightened by wonderful stories that my mother read to me and the special culinary treats she served me, particularly easy-to-digest dishes like puddings. It was never fun to be sick, but there was a bright side. And the impact of those times will extend into eternity because of the talks my mother and I had and the stories that I heard, both

Puddings and Custards • 180–187

from an endless variety of books and from my mother's own life experiences growing up on a farm in Wisconsin.

As an adult I've learned that entertaining children is fun, and it can also provide profound nurturing opportunities; for serving children food of any kind is an appropriate and painless opportunity to teach manners. Sitting in a lovely tearoom having lunch with my mother at age five, I thought it was fun to learn the proper use of a soup spoon. At five it felt special. At ten years of age, at the family dinner table, it might not have been as enjoyable. At ten it would have felt like just another rule.

Even earlier than that, my friends and I had tea parties in the backyard, serving small triangular pieces of cinnamon toast and tiny cups of cold lemonade. We shared our "tea" with a doll, and even a cat and dog became honored guests for as long as they would stay still. We learned of the niceties of "taking tea." The table had a white cloth and was set with blue and white porcelain doll dishes and small pieces of cutlery. We also learned the fun of "dress-up tea." The doll was dressed in her best, and my friend and I pretended to dress as grand ladies. We learned that you couldn't do some things in play clothes; you had to dress up to make them work.

Children dressed in play clothes behave differently than those dressed in party clothes. A formal table setting evokes different behavior as well as different expectations from guests.

HELPING CHILDREN GIVE THE GIFT OF HOSPITALITY

The early years of a child's life are precious. It is a time when there is much to learn, and children are eager to absorb these lessons. Wait too long and that eagerness disappears. One of those lessons is that hospitality extends beyond just receiving. Childhood is a wonderful time to start to defeat the attitude of me-ism and cultivate an attitude of knowing how to give. Indeed, it is more blessed to give than to receive.

Children can give a unique gift to the elderly by just their presence; and, in return, the elderly have a lifetime of experience to share with even the very young. A plate of cookies for a shut-in neighbor, a handmade gingerbread cookie Christmas ornament to decorate the tree of a friend, a scribbled note or a hand-drawn picture for someone who is lonely: all these are simple acts of hos-

Gingerbread Christmas Tree Ornaments • 170

pitality that children can perform. Except for unusual circumstances, children should not be isolated from the elderly or the handicapped. People with mixed needs, backgrounds, and ages have much to offer each other.

Shortly after our family first moved to California from Chicago, we began to attend a large church in downtown Los Angeles. After church we sometimes walked several blocks through the downtown area to a cafeteria that had seemingly endless choices of foods. On our way we almost always encountered a street beggar (they weren't called *the homeless* in those days). Indelibly etched upon my memory is the image of my father sharing what he had with someone who asked him for help. Sometimes he gave money; sometimes he bought the person a cup of hot coffee. It was never much because we didn't have much ourselves. But my father never turned anyone away. He never treated another human being as though he were not worth noticing. And he never handed anyone a religious tract instead of food when the person was hungry.

That another person's need brought to my door becomes my obligation was a lesson I learned early, just by watching my parents.

Issues revolving around food seem to generate major conflicts between kids and their parents—and even between the children themselves. There are times to say a firm "No" in my opinion, even though many experts would disagree. Then if the child disobeys, he or she must be punished. But all of that sometimes can be avoided.

Two children in the back seat of a car were arguing over which fast food place to go for lunch. Susan, the mother, had promised the children a fast food treat on this their last day of school. Since they didn't often get fast food, this treat had been anticipated with joy and fought over intensely. Rather than trying to convince one child that the other child's choice was better or, worse still, getting food from both places so that no one would be unhappy, Susan decisively informed them that they were going to a place she had chosen. But they had a choice, too, she said. They could continue to argue and whine about their mother's decision and go home to peanut butter sandwiches, or they could have their special lunch where she chose to take them. They chose the treat!

Kids aren't stupid. After they get used to this "guided choice" approach, they usually begin to choose wisely. Parent and child are both spared the anger and exhaustion of trying to win. In these situations, the key to success lies in following certain basic principles.

Set up the choice in a way that makes it likely the child will choose what you want him to choose (in this instance, to stop fighting so you can take them to lunch).

Don't act as if the result is a punishment but rather a result of the child's choice ("you can choose to go to a restaurant of my choice or you can choose to go home").

The child never has a right to choose to disobey, but every human being at any age already makes many daily choices that have consequences. Children, however, often aren't aware of the results of their behavior until it's too late. Framing certain demands in a way that emphasizes choice and consequences is one way to teach a child good behavior.

The last thing a parent wants is to turn the evening meal into a major battlefield. A choice between drinking milk and having dessert (as opposed to no milk, no dessert) can often work—but only if it is framed within the structure of a choice. You can say: "You have a choice: you can choose to drink your milk and have ice cream, or you can choose to leave your milk and have no dessert" as opposed to "Drink your milk or you can't have dessert." The first way results in the child taking responsibility for his or her actions. The second way pits the parent against the child and almost invites disobedience.

Children can't always be given choices. Sometimes the parent must say no. But when you can use the choice method, and issues over food are a good place to start, you empower your child to choose wisely and to build self-confidence.

Not long ago a patient told me about her teenage daughter who, because she was not allowed to go out one night, angrily threw her dinner across the room. I felt, as I do so often in my counseling experience, that there is a vast difference between cultivating a good self-image and indulging gross selfishness. Indeed, good behavior fosters good self-esteem. Even we Christians get it confused. A person with a good self-image is confident enough to be free from himself and to thus forget himself. Self-forgetfulness, not self-preoccupation, is the end result of high self-esteem. Only when I am truly comfortable with myself can I forget myself and care about others.

Through experiences of hospitality, the very young can learn how to have fun, how to mark the significant events of life, how to develop and use these safety zones of refurbishment, and also how to minister to others. A child who feels loved and cared about, yet not overindulged, will quickly gain self-confidence and can then be encouraged to reach out to others.

I will never forget my first day at school. I was a shy child to start with. Then, because of adult problems with paperwork, I was late. I remember standing just inside the open door to the classroom, all alone, wanting to run home. All the children were sitting in a circle on the floor, and they all turned to look at me as I stood there.

The teacher's name was Mrs. Black, and her personality fit her name. She didn't say a word to me. But a girl who lived across the street from me jumped up, ran over to where I stood, grabbed my hand, and said: "Come over here and sit with us." With relief I followed her.

A simple act of kindness saved the day for me.

The gesture was hospitality on its most rudimentary level. It was the offering of kindness to another human being—in this instance, from one child to another. With children or adults, this is the meaning of the biblical command to be given to hospitality.

Are you willing to stoop down and consider the needs and desires of little children; to remember the weaknesses and loneliness of people who are growing old, to stop asking how much your friends love you, and to ask yourself whether you love them enough; to bear in mind the things that other people have to bear on their hearts; to trim your lamp so that it will give more light and less smoke, and to carry it in front of you so that your shadow will fall behind you; to make a grave for your ugly thoughts and a garden for your kindly feelings, with the gate open? Are you willing to do these things for a day? Then you are ready to keep Christmas!

HENRY VAN DYKE

❦ E·I·G·H·T

The Christmas Hearth

Late Christmas afternoon the phone rang. The person on the other end of the line spoke with a small voice, consistent with her five years of age. "Everyone's angry with me," Karen said, with an obvious attempt to hold back her tears. "They think I'm not happy."

Karen had been adopted a few months before Christmas, after an emotional court battle, and I remembered my most recent conversation with her adoptive mother. In their desire to help Karen adjust to their home, the adoptive family had put a great emphasis on Christmas, telling her what a wonderful time she would have. They planned to give her expensive gifts, and they eagerly anticipated her reaction.

In her desire to please her new family, yet still lonely for the foster family where she had been for almost five years, Karen had slipped into a Christmas depression. After all, she barely knew these people, yet felt the demand of Christmas was to "be happy!" It was a demand that immediately removed any chance for happiness, since happiness is an elusive thing that dissipates when it becomes a goal. The result was this frantic phone call to me to find out what was the matter.

Predictably, the day after Christmas was a happy one for Karen. All expectations for her happiness were gone, and she relaxed and began to enjoy the season—and, of course, the presents.

Holidays in general, and Christmas in particular, are perfect times for offering hospitality. They abound with potential for decorating. Furthermore, Christmas is filled with meaning, particularly for those of us who have a religious commitment.

Yet Christmas depression, or holiday depression, is not limited to five-year-olds. Nor does it necessarily indicate pathology. Indeed, it can result from a myriad of causes. Christmas can be bleak for some adults because it seems that nothing can match happier childhood holidays. Or unhappy holidays in childhood can predispose a person to feel that joy is not to be part of that person's adult experience.

For most of us, the amount of joy holidays bring varies from year to year. For myself, for example, Christmas in childhood was an experience that was difficult to duplicate as an adult.

The anticipation of the arrival of the aunts and uncles with their huge bags of mysteriously shaped parcels; the songs sung around the piano; the wonderful aroma of food cooking in the kitchen; the nativity scene, which was carefully placed in the cotton that lay around the base of the tree: these combined to remind me in a deep, almost mystical way of the love of God.

Suspicion that there might be a man dressed in red, riding a sleigh pulled by reindeer, kept alive my childish need for something magical. Yet I never remember confusing the myth of Santa Claus with the reality of the Incarnation.

I never sensed family closeness more keenly than on Christmas Eve when, according to Swedish custom, we ate traditional foods and opened presents. The food came before we opened presents, and thus was never quite properly appreciated. Yet the tradition set by those foods has remained with me throughout the years, long after most of those who were then present have gone on to be with the Lord. The herring, which my father carefully pickled each year, was served along with a choice of various sausages and cheeses, jellied veal (or Sylta), rice pudding, and potato sausage—which was made from scratch in my mother's day. Added to these were Aunt Lydia's Molded Salad, Aunt Esther's Coconut Layer Cake (see index) and, topping them all, my mother's wonderful Swedish cookies, cut into a variety of shapes and sizes, sprinkled with colored sugar and served with Princess Charlotte Pudding (see index) or with the more traditional Scandinavian pudding.

**Jellied Veal
(Kalv Sylta)** • 195

Lydia's Molded Salad • 202

**Betty's Scandinavian
Pudding** • 181

Nutty Pumpkin Bread • 133

The inevitable lutefisk (codfish soaked in lye, dried and then cooked and served with a white sauce) was, and still is, a must on every truly traditional Swedish Christmas Eve table. Since everyone in my family who liked it is gone, lutefisk is no longer a part of our Christmas Eve. But the other dishes remain, and remind me each year of wonderful past Christmases as well as of the special people who made them. The food, and the tradition that surrounds the preparation and the serving of that food, is a safety zone at this special time of year. It becomes both a comfort and an encouragement as it reminds me of a wonderful past and heritage that provide motivation for the future.

For me, the joy of those childhood Christmases—particularly the peace I felt late on Christmas Eve, curled up on the sofa in my traditional gift of new pajamas, looking at the blinking, colored lights on the tree—could be duplicated at no other time of year. I felt as though the happiness could never go away.

Yet in the adult years that have followed. I have experienced a great many different Christmases. Christmas has brought joy in a kind of rushed, busy way in the years when I've tried to be in two or more places in order to celebrate with those I love. It was infused with sorrow the year that a Christmas wreath and poinsettia plants were the tokens of warmth at my father's funeral, one week before Christmas Eve, rather than signs of festivity in a happy home. And after losing my mother and other close family members all in one year, the only way to survive at all that Christmas was to focus on others and provide Christmas for some foster children.

Of course, not all people have had such wonderful traditions in their past that integrate childhood with adulthood in a positive way. Yet all through our lives we build memories for the future, and, as adults, we create traditions for ourselves and others. So don't be afraid to add new ideas and foods to mix with the old. It is impossible for me to write about holiday feasting this year without sharing two recipes that my daughter, Rayne, found from the ancient past and reinvented for her own use. Suffice it to say that after tasting her Sweet Potato Puff, sweet potatoes, which have never been a favorite of mine, are now something I will look forward to. And pumpkin pie, which is a personal favorite, has now a new dimension with Rayne's Creamy Pumpkin Pie.

Sweet Potato Puff • 150

Creamy Pumpkin Pie • 179

And for anyone, no matter how bleak the past, this Christmas can be the first year of positive traditions that will extend into the years ahead and will provide a safety zone of hospitality for young and old alike. Build a memory for your own children. Create a tradition for yourself. Establish a pattern of hospitality that will provide a place for others—a refuge from the cold darkness of the world beyond the hearth.

Grief and loss do not respect time. For those who are single, widowed, or set aside by illness, the very sense of happiness that people exude at Christmas can, by contrast, be depressing. If you are in grief or ill, quiet Christmases can be uplifting. Decorate with candles and fill the background with inspiring music such as *The Messiah* or hymns—and don't avoid people altogether. If you are single, accept invitations to the festivities of others; and, even better, invite others into your own home. Have an open house and serve finger foods, or invite a small number of people (even one is enough) for a Christmas dinner. Use some of the shortcuts presented in this book, like one-dish meals, and provide some of the tasty snack foods, such as Nut Brittle or Popcorn Balls (see index). Don't forget, loneliness is one of the biggest emotional problems our society faces. And Christmas seems to intensify it by its expectation of happiness.

Christmas 2001, after the bombing of the Twin Towers in New York and the Pentagon in Washington, DC, was an unusual blend of melancholy, grief, and joy for America as a nation. For those of us who didn't lose anyone directly, Christmas happiness was subdued—and yet the old and trusted symbols were comforting. I found myself valuing family and friends just a little more than before. I used a smaller tree with fewer toy ornaments and added several patriotic ornaments. Rather than decorating with a lot of Santa Clauses and snowmen, once again, as after my mother's death, I used more candles and floral arrangements, this time of red berries and leaves touched with gold glitter. The American flag still hung in my window.

COMFORT STOCKINGS 🌲

Christmas 2001 was also the year that we as a family established a new tradition. Comfort Stockings are what we call them, and they offer a form of hospitality to those who have less than we do, or for those experiencing grief or loss. Since then Comfort Stockings have become something we do for a variety of other reasons. They have come to mean, "You're Special."

In 2001 we chose two families who were economically struggling and made Christmas stockings for each person according to his or her need. For example, a child who had a long ride to school on a bicycle received, among other things, a warm pair of gloves. A teenage girl for whom there would be no chance for extras that Christmas received a bracelet and some makeup in her stocking. Her mother found perfume and her father got a flashlight/radio. There were other things, too, some practical and some not so practical. And for each person there was Christmas candy and, for some, candy bars. On this occasion, we also included gifts that did not fit in stockings: warm nightgowns for two people who were without heat; art supplies for an aspiring artist; a game, and practical gifts like soap and small food items for those who needed them.

It was important to make these stockings as unto the Lord, which meant using quality items. As we planned our Comfort Stockings, I was reminded of missionary Amy Carmichael's words, as she instructed the children at Dohnavur Fellowship in South India to always clean behind the furniture where no earthly eye would see but the angels would know. And I thought of Mother Teresa who, as she cleaned the putrefying wounds of those who came to her for help, saw only that she was doing it for Christ Himself.

Matthew 25:34–40 resonated in our minds: "Then shall the King say unto them on his right hand, Come, ye blessed of my Father, inherit the kingdom prepared for you from the foundation of the world: For I was an hungred, and ye gave me meat: I was thirsty, and ye gave me drink: I was a stranger, and ye took me in:

Naked, and ye clothed me: I was sick, and ye visited me: I was in prison, and ye came unto me. Then shall the righteous answer him, saying, Lord, when saw we thee an hungred, and fed thee? or thirsty, and gave thee drink? When saw we thee a stranger, and took thee in? or naked, and clothed thee? Or when saw we thee sick, or in prison, and came unto thee? And the King shall answer and say unto them, Verily I say unto you, Inasmuch as ye have done it unto one of the least of these my brethren, ye have done it unto me" (KJV).

It is not only the poor who can be helped by something as simple as a Comfort Stocking. A pregnant woman, for example, who has lost her husband or who has no husband, can be encouraged about that small life soon to be born by the gift of a stocking. Decorate it appropriately and put in baby supplies and toys and something personal for the mother, like a locket that can hold a picture, or a picture frame, or a small baby "brag" photo album. A gift certificate, a book, perfume or lipstick, body cream, a special candle, and, of course, Christmas candy can be added touches that personalize the stocking.

Stockings for people in particular need of this kind of hospitality at this time of year could be sent to military personnel who are far from home, to an elderly person who lives alone or in a convalescent home, to someone recently bereaved, to a student who can't get home for the holidays, to those who are ill, or to someone who has lost a job.

"Be appropriate" is the important rule to remember. If someone has been bereaved, a stocking with more muted colors is better than a bright red one with "Ho! Ho! Ho!" on it.

Personalize your gifts. If a person likes to scrapbook, you might add stickers. If a child collects small porcelain dogs, add one. If a man likes to play tape cassettes in his car, include one. And remember, no one is too old for a stocking.

Try to include at least one main item of value: a silver bracelet for a teenager, a nail polish set or bath set for a woman, an inexpensive novelty watch or a tool for a man. Above all, never give anything that has been used unless you're handing down a family heirloom to a grandchild!

Everybody likes a stocking. Usually at Christmas I get books, small gifts, and cards from certain publishers for whom I have written. The first year I published with Discovery House, I received a package from them not long before Christmas. It was early evening when the package was delivered, so I sat down by my lighted tree and opened it. To my surprise, inside was a blue furry stocking with a white cuff. At that point in my relationship with the company, I wasn't aware of all that they produced, so the CDs and books were a nice way to find out, and I enjoyed the candies as I listened and read. Making the gift personal was a Christmas CD card signed by all the editorial staff. This stocking arrived at a time when I was feeling a bit overwhelmed and discouraged, so it was a gift of cheer on a not-so-cheerful day.

God loves to give His children a special comfort, and to do that He often uses us, His other children. Comfort Stockings are one way to do this as we offer hospitality to others.

CHRISTMAS COOKIES

They were called gingerbread boys then. Not gingerbread boys and girls. Certainly not gingerbread persons! With their raisin buttons and jaunty frosting hats and boots, they were gingerbread *boys*.

The year was around 1945. It was Christmas. At school, plans were being made for the class Christmas party, and I impulsively volunteered my mother's Christmas cookies. Predictably, she came through for me. I knew she would!

But she didn't just make cookies. She made gingerbread boys—twenty-nine of them! Each one looked fat and proud, ready to burst his plump raisin buttons. My mother covered the gingerbread boys, individually, with a clear wrap so that they became small Christmas gifts for each member of my class. Most of the children just looked at these creations for a while before they bravely broke off a foot or gingerly nibbled at an arm. It was the 1940s, before the time of commercial cookies and elaborate, gaudy decorations. For most of my classmates, this was a major and unique treat. And I was star of the class for a day!

Whether it is gingerbread boys or frosted stars and snowmen, Christmas celebrations don't seem complete without Christmas cookies.

Cookies are small, flat, sweet cakes baked in the oven on a thin baking sheet. They vary in type from a small portion of dough dropped on a cookie sheet to cutout cookies, which are frosted with designs or sprinkled with colored sugar, to all sorts of variations in between. Some cookies are soft and thick, while others are valued for their thinness and crispness. Some are filled with nuts, raisins, or various jellies and jams.

Many cookies originated in countries like Sweden, Denmark, Norway, Germany, France, and England. In some countries they are called biscuits, from a French word meaning "twice-cooked." The name comes from a hard biscuit that was cooked twice and then used by the Roman soldiers as a food staple several centuries ago. Appropriately, Louis XIV called it "stone bread." From "stone bread" we have derived our present-day cookie.

Following the development of the cookie has come an end-less variety of whimsical cookie jars, cookie cutters, and even cookie molds. People sell cookies in little shops along the street. And cookies are served in every conceivable manner, either huge and by themselves, or as a delicate accompaniment to a frozen dessert or a cup of afternoon tea.

The modern cookie or biscuit is definitely here to stay. And the most important cookie of all is the Christmas cookie, which brings its own built-in potential for tradition. Making Christmas cookies can be a wonderful childhood activity. Yes, it's easier to bake without children underfoot. But what better way is there to teach baking skills and spend quality time together at the same time? What better way is there to build a memory?

Christmas cookies can be used in many other ways, too. Heaped on a plate and served with a cup of coffee, they provide a genuine offering of hospitality. Placed on a Christmas plate and tied up with brightly colored ribbon, they become a treat to a shut-in or an elderly person.

Christmas Cookies • 165–176

Packed carefully in a Christmas tin, they can be mailed to a student away at college or a relative in another state or a homesick son or daughter serving in the military and stationed far away from home.

Christmas cookies, arranged in colorful variety on a large, painted china plate, are always served in my home at Christmas Eve dinner. For a Swede like myself, Christmas is simply not Christmas without Pepparkakor Christmas trees with their green-sugared branches and the eager, bright-eyed gingerbread boys with their plump, raisin buttons.

SPECIAL CONSIDERATIONS FOR HOLIDAY HOSPITALITY

No matter how hard we try to duplicate that perfect Christmas from the past, or produce a new, even more perfect one in the present, we usually can't. We ourselves are different each year. Our circumstances are different. Furthermore, whenever we focus on happiness we are sure to be disappointed, for trying to be happy is a sure way to lose that happiness.

Some basic principles, however, if followed, can make the difference between a Christmas that epitomizes hospitality at its best and a Christmas that ends up being a catastrophe of exhaustion and depression. First of all, don't believe all the *Ho! Ho! Ho!* hype out there. Don't be discouraged if the TV kitchens look marvelously neat and well equipped, while yours is a disaster. Don't believe that you are supposed to look rested after a day of battling the crowds in your local shopping mall. You can, however, ease the pressure by using foods such as Turkey Meatloaf , Chicken Tortilla Casserole, and other one-dish meals that have been prepared ahead and frozen (see index).

Incidentally, have you ever noticed that all the great make-it-yourself gift ideas come out in magazines and newspapers just a few weeks, or even days, before Christmas? Now if you're really going to make Aunt Nellie a hand-knit sweater you'd better start in July, not December. And if all your gifts are going to be foods that are homemade, ideas in the Sunday edition of the newspaper two days before Christmas are not going to help you much, even if they *are* labeled "last-minute gifts that are easy to make." The unfortunate truth is, even if we *don't* try to make these last-minute miracle gifts, we somehow feel we should be able to. After all, it wouldn't be in print if it weren't possible, would it?

Consistent with not attempting the impossible is the need to simplify and make choices. Don't try to do it all. One Christmas a few years back my challenge was to simplify. I had a last-minute writing job that had a very high priority. So for the first time in my adult life I gave up my responsibility for the Christmas Eve celebration and handed it over to a friend, knowing that this year it would not be Swedish. We also cut down on the number of activities as well as the number of guests. Then, at the last minute, my friend got sick.

As I rushed to the Swedish delicatessen, *simplify* was still my motto. Some things could be left out, and I would have to give up some of my perfectionism. When the delicatessen was sold out of the traditional Swedish potato sausage, rather than trying to rush back the next day, I settled (with some discomfort) for a different kind of sausage. I hadn't had time to bake as much that year, so I mixed store-bought cookies with home-baked ones. Perhaps as a result of simplifying and the consequent relaxation, I have rarely felt such warmth as I did in that small Christmas Eve gathering. I was more free to focus on people, which is, of course, the essence of true hospitality. And I don't believe that since childhood I have ever been as aware of Christ and His birth on the day of that birth as I was that year. Simplifying meant time to think, to worship, and to share the love of Christ with others.

When it comes to a complicated, more extended period of hospitality like Christmas, *organization* is almost as critical as simplifying. I find that keeping an ongoing list all year long helps in my Christmas shopping. I don't actively look for gifts all year long, but if I find that perfect gift at a good price, I don't hesitate to buy it, even if it is July. This doesn't work, however, unless the item and the name of the person the gift is for are carefully written down on a list, which is then put where you can find it immediately. Otherwise, rather than being able to buy wisely and thoughtfully, you will buy several times over for one person and not buy at all for another.

As the Christmas season approaches, important decisions have to be made: how much baking to do, how much to entertain, and who to invite. *Choices* need to be deliberate. For example, no one should try to prepare a Christmas Eve feast and also cook a big dinner on Christmas Day. Even seemingly small things can become a matter of choice. This year, for example, I reinvented an old popcorn ball recipe that my mother used to make. Then, when someone said the popcorn balls wouldn't freeze well, they became something I would have to make right before Christmas. So I had a choice: drop something else I was going to prepare right before Christmas, and substitute popcorn balls, or make popcorn balls another year. (Since then I've discovered that the popcorn balls freeze very well!)

Popcorn Balls • 154

Remember, the holidays should be times of worship and praise, as well as times of fun and refurbishment. You can't have fun when you are overwhelmed by soul-sapping fatigue. You can't worship and praise if you are too distracted to focus on the spiritual dimension of Christmas.

Ideally, if you have Thanksgiving at your home, someone else should have Christmas dinner. Such an arrangement frees you to try something innovative for whatever holiday you are hosting. Again, choice, along with simplification and organization, makes possible an added activity or two. A Christmas tree decorating party, featuring snack foods and Christmas music, can provide good fun for a group of friends—and can also help you get your tree decorated. (If you do this, be sure to have your tree ready to decorate and your more breakable ornaments already on the tree before your guests arrive.)

A Christmas card party, where everyone brings his or her Christmas cards and writes them out together, can take the monotony out of a job that many people dread. Again, combining a variety of snacks and a group of congenial people can make this time both profitable and fun. Having card tables set up ahead of time and choosing appropriate background music are organizational-type helps. Having a supply of blank paper, extra pens, attractive seals, and other useful miscellany can provide a special touch of hospitality.

When I taught school, I always tried to have something to fall back on just in case the lesson I had planned for the day didn't take the whole period. That kind of planning—organizing beyond what you need—is also a good idea for any act of hospitality, especially one as complicated as Christmas. Gifts of coloring books and crayons for the young will help keep them occupied while the adults enjoy each other. Serving dinner to children at a separate table, with their own décor and more durable table settings, alleviates adult nervousness and makes the occasion special for the children involved. An extra present of candy or a book can come in handy for an unexpected guest. Providing large trash bags for guests means you don't have to spend time later in the day cleaning up.

Time, as well as things and people, needs to be organized. The years when the main Christmas festivities are at someone else's home are good years to spend more time with your children in helping them learn something about the meaning of Christian hospitality.

Making ornaments together, teaching children how to bake, and then helping them think of places to share what they have made can be enjoyable and instructive. Older people in convalescent homes enjoy visits from children and teenagers, as do older couples or single people and those who are ill but at home. A cup of hot chocolate and some homemade bread offered to a homeless person, along with warm gloves or a blanket, could be counted as fulfilling the scriptural promise that in doing something for those who need it most we do it unto Him whose birthday we celebrate. All of these are types of hospitality.

Organizing time should also include setting time aside to relax. Last year I bought myself a book of Christmas mystery stories. Reading, especially reading mysteries, is one way I have of relaxing. Each night before I went to sleep I read one of those stories. As I did, I forgot about the demands of the day and, as a result, slept better. It was my own time by myself. Sitting quietly watching the tree lights, indulging in a long bubble bath or hot shower, curling up in a chair with a warm robe and slippers: these are just a few ways to use a small piece of time to recover oneself and prepare to once again minister to others.

Sometimes a single, small organizational act will make a big difference in how we feel. On Christmas Day when we have dinner with friends, I'm usually tired, since my big time of responsibility for hospitality falls on Christmas Eve each year. As I was getting ready to leave for dinner this past Christmas, I impulsively turned back my bed, fluffed the pillows, and laid out a book to read. It took only a minute to leave the room looking inviting, and when I came home it was a welcome sight. This example seems almost too trivial to mention. But such small acts of pampering oneself in the middle of major demands can become significant in our own physical, and spiritual, refreshment and refurbishment.

CHERISH TRADITIONS: OLD AND NEW 🎄

Christmas, above all other times of the year, is a chance to cherish the old and initiate the new. This year my daughter gave me a beautiful, hand-blown, glass ornament from Poland. It is shaped in the form of a shell and is signed by the man who made it. It is new now, but someday it will be an old and cherished token of the past, perhaps for her or her children. On that same tree hangs a circular-shaped, plastic ornament with a windmill-like center, which revolves from the heat of a nearby Christmas light. I can remember that ornament from as far back as I remember Christmas trees. Its earthly value is probably zero, but I wouldn't sell it for any amount of money. My tree comforts me each year in its blending of the very old, the very new, and all sorts of memories in between.

Traditional occasions, things, foods, presents: all of these add to the feeling of comfort, the sense of the hearth, that is the very essence of hospitality. In my economizing of time one Christmas I decided to buy a fancy ice cream dessert instead of making my traditional Scandinavian pudding. Proud of my ability to give up tradition in order to gain time, I told someone about my plan. Spontaneously he replied, "You mean we're not going to have the pudding this year?" Then he quickly added, "That's OK. Don't worry about it." But I did worry about it! It wasn't that much effort to make the pudding since it's an easy recipe. I simply hadn't realized that apart from my own early family memories anyone else felt that sentimental about it. Sometimes shared traditions become traditions for others. Such traditions bind people together and make certain special times of hospitality even more meaningful.

FOCUS BEYOND YOURSELF 🌲

Perhaps the biggest liability of major holidays like Christmas and Thanksgiving is the loneliness and depression they can create. Like the little girl at the beginning of this chapter, we try too hard to be happy. *Happy* seems to be the demand of the season, and sometimes in our attempts to be happy we become totally selfish.

Children learn these things early in life. This year a young boy who had received an abundance of gifts for Christmas came into my office. Michael's gifts had been expensive, while his brother's had been less costly. For that reason Michael had received fewer gifts than his brother, but their gifts had been equal in value. Michael understood this. Yet as he counted his gifts and saw that his brother had received more, he began to pout. When the difference in value was explained to him, this child of ten chose not to understand—and his attitude paid off. Intimidated by accusations of unfairness, his parents quickly went out and bought him more gifts. Of course, then the other child felt bad. For Michael, Christmas is not a time to worship God, even though his parents are Christians. Christmas is not even a time to give. Christmas is a time to get things, a time to have fun and be happy. Yet he was miserable throughout the holiday season. Nothing was ever quite enough. The tree wasn't big enough. There wasn't enough candy. Certainly there were not enough gifts.

An obscure little book called *Sartor Resartus* by the English essayist Thomas Carlyle influenced me deeply as a student. In essence the book states that if we reduce our expectations to zero, then anything above that zero mark becomes happiness. If I expect few gifts, many gifts are an unexpected joy. If I expect to be alone on Christmas, then a visitor brings great happiness to me. If I focus on the happiness I can provide for others, then those good things that people do for me will be unexpected and joyful.

In contrast, many families I see in counseling are intense about having the perfect Christmas, as though it were an inherent right. Consistent with that emphasis, they resent anyone who threatens to spoil that expectation. The ill, the poor, the aged, the unlikable are shunned, lest they spoil Christmas. Yet their

Christmas is spoiled before it starts by expectations that are impossible to fulfill.

Because of the extra pressure on me the year I had the book deadline, I knew I couldn't even try to do it all. In fact, I wasn't sure I could do any of it. A few days before Christmas I committed the Christmas hospitality problem to God and asked for His priorities and organization in a way I had not done at any other holiday season. After that I had a peace about what was important and what was not. And God answered in other special ways. People helped unexpectedly. The writing was finished on time. And the occasions of hospitality were the warmest ever.

Christmas is a time to do special things for people we love. It is a time for building and enjoying traditions that, in the long run, bind families and friends together. It is a time for mysterious bundles and expressions of love. It is an occasion for festive decorations and bright, happy colors and lights. It is a time to extend the warmth of our own personal hearth to those who are outside in the cold.

Christmas is also a time to remember that the greatest gift this old earth has ever received was given in a stable built to house animals, in a town that had no room for the King of kings. 🌲

In a perfect friendship... each member of the circle feels, in his secret heart, humbled before all the rest. Sometimes he wonders what he is doing there among his betters. He is lucky beyond dessert to be in such company. Especially when the whole group is together, each bringing out all that is best, wisest, or funniest in all the others. Those are the golden sessions; when four or five of us after a hard day's walking have come to our inn; when our slippers are on, our feet spread out towards the blaze and our drinks at our elbows; when the whole world, and something beyond the world, opens itself to our minds as we talk; ... while at the same time an Affection mellowed by the years enfolds us. Life—natural life—has no better gift to give.

C. S. LEWIS

I Love Coffee, I Love Tea

After learning of the death of his wife and two daughters, Anne Frank's father settled into life with the family of Miep Gies, the woman who had helped hide the Frank family in her attic. Miep and her husband were his family now.

Shops in Holland were empty. Food was scarce. Luxury was almost nonexistent. One day a package from America arrived for Mr. Frank. Among other things, the package contained three small packets. Mr. Frank handed them to Miep to open.

In her book *Anne Frank Remembered,* Miep describes that moment:

> The first I opened sent an aroma of cocoa up into my face. It was overwhelming. I felt the texture, so soft and powdery, the color so dark brown.
>
> Seeing it and smelling the cocoa, I began to cry.
>
> Otto said, "Take it, make it."
>
> I couldn't stop crying. It was unbelievable to me that I was seeing real cocoa again.[1]

For Miep and her family and friends, food had so often been both the measure and the cause of sharp emotions. During the German occupation, the scarcity of food in Holland made it very difficult for Miep and her husband to feed the Frank family and others who were in hiding. Yet often a scrap of extra food, a cake made by saving certain staples out of their ordinary meals, had been used to make just another dull day in hiding into a special day.

Telling of those early days of the German occupation, Miep describes making a meager meal from a few carrots and small potatoes. The food was simple, and there was not enough of it. Yet during one of the bleakest times, a good strong pot of coffee, shared by Miep and her husband with a neighbor-couple as they secretly listened to the BBC, recharged their courage. The neighbor delivered her baby that night, and all of them felt once again like going on.

For Miep and her family and friends, a sense of encouragement seemed to arise from these times of sharing food, and particularly from conversations over a cup of coffee.

One night, shortly before they were to sit down to their meager dinner, they heard the welcome news that Germany had been defeated. "We sat down to eat our meal feeling such joy that we stopped being aware of the gnawing hunger in our bellies," says Miep. "The food tasted like the most marvellous meal I'd ever eaten."[2]

After the war ended, while Otto Frank was still living with Miep and her husband, it was over a cup of coffee with friends that Mr. Frank was persuaded to publish Anne's diary. Initially he had felt that the diary was too private to publish. But he was gradually persuaded that the voice of a young person in hiding during those times was important to share with the world. And how much richer the world has been for that decision.

For centuries, coffee and tea have been at the center of most safety zones that involve food of any kind. The fondness that the

English have for afternoon tea is reflected in the children's rhyme, "Polly Put the Kettle On":

> Blow the fire and make the toast,
> Put the muffins down to roast,
> Blow the fire and make the toast,
> We'll all have tea.

In showing the impact that both tea and coffee have had on the civilized world, the old Mother Goose counting-out rhyme says it simply:

> One, two, three,
> I love coffee,
> And Billy loves tea.

Eventually the rhyme was chanted during my childhood in the following form:

> I love coffee,
> I love tea,
> I love the boys,
> And the boys love me.

Because of the place coffee and tea have had throughout the centuries, fine china and vast, complicated rituals have been created for their service.

In 1823 the English essayist Charles Lamb wrote of what he called his "partiality for old china." He describes the "little, flawless, azure-tinctured grotesques, that under the notion of men and women, float about, uncircumscribed by any element, in that world before perspective—a china tea-cup." Lamb goes on to refer to a specific purchase that gave him and his sister, with whom he lived, much joy: "a set of extraordinary old blue china . . . which we were now for the first time using." In talking about the designs and figures painted on his china-cups he refers to them as "my old friends."

High up in my cabinet I, too, have a set of "old friends," cups and saucers that my maternal grandmother used when she served coffee for someone's birthday or for other special occasions. I am sure that they have little monetary value. Yet when I even pick up one of those cups and saucers I remember wonderful times and wonderful people: family members who are now drinking out of heavenly chalices.

A lovely custom handed down from my Swedish ancestors, and comparable in part to English tea, is an event called a kaffebord. The word *kaffebord* means, quite literally, coffee table. A formal kaffebord can celebrate almost any occasion, from a wedding to a graduation. More important, it provides a time for friends to get together.

For a true kaffebord, large quantities of good, strong coffee, a bowl full of sugar cubes, and a pitcher of rich cream are essential. Colorful bowls of fresh flowers, the best china and crystal in the house, and a lovely tablecloth provide the backdrop for a time of joy and intimacy. This is one of those times to use family heirlooms and bright colors.

The food served at a true kaffebord consists primarily of desserts. These should include at the very least a yeast coffee cake, a plain cake, and a fancy, filled cake, finishing with a variety of cookies.

Apart from a formal kaffebord, even a simple cup of coffee served attractively with or without coffeecake or cookies will pick up most people's spirits. Our church has a coffee table with coffee and baked goods available after the morning service on Sundays. One Sunday I was involved in a conversation several feet away from the table. Cold weather had come after an unseasonable hot spell, and I had not brought a coat, so I was chilly. From what seemed to be out of nowhere someone handed me a plain paper cup filled with coffee. As the hot fluid trickled down my throat, I felt warmed and refreshed; and that simple cup of hot coffee nurtured a longer and more productive conversation.

I was first introduced to coffee as something to ward off the cold. As a child I was not allowed to have coffee or tea, and I always envied the adults as they drank their delicious-smelling hot coffee. It smelled so good and they seemed to enjoy it so much.

Then one day my mother and I went to the ocean with Aunt Esther and Uncle Blanton. It was a cold, foggy day. As we sat on the bluff overlooking the ocean we shivered in the cold mist that was coming from the sea.

Aunt Esther brought out her big Thermos bottle of hot coffee. As she poured the hot liquid into the china cups she had brought for the occasion and noticed me shivering in the cold, she asked: "Can't Elizabeth have some, too?"

My mother gave her consent. I was so elated that I forgot I was cold. I was joining the adult world, if only for a few minutes. Furthermore, I was sure that I was in for a very special treat. As I took my first trusting sip of the hot—and by the time I got it, milky—liquid, I luxuriated in the warmth. But the taste! I couldn't figure out how something that smelled so good could taste so awful.

After that experience, I never drank coffee on a regular basis until I taught school and needed a pickup in the middle of the day. Then I learned to love coffee with as much enthusiasm as my Scandinavian ancestors.

No matter how elaborate the foods that are served, ultimately just basic coffee and tea seem to be mainstays of the psychological equilibrium of civilization. For,

> If all the world were apple-pie
> And all the sea were ink;
> And all the trees were bread and cheese,
> What would we do for drink?

In comparison to tea, rituals in connection with coffee seem simple indeed. Taking tea can be a fairly structured event that demands time. All this ceremony is like a comma in the middle of a sentence that says, "slow down," or "pause." In *Having Tea,* Catherine Calvert comments:

> Not the least of teatime's pleasures is the ceremony it serves up and the satisfaction of doing something as it has been done for generations. This was the spoon Great-Grandmother used, this was the way we had our cinnamon toast, cut in soldiers or in butterflies, tea served in *this* cup was the magic cure for measles, winter colds, homesickness—all speak of family love.[3]

Children enjoy being included in the ritual of taking tea and will enjoy the comfort as well as the making of childhood memories. For everyone concerned, cinnamon toast and tea is always a good combination.

Even by itself toast conveys the feeling of the hearth. Charles Dickens refers to this feeling in his *Pickwick Papers:* "The fire was blazing brightly under the influence of the bellows, and the kettle was singing gayly. . . . A small tray of tea things was arranged on the table, a plate of hot buttered toast was gently simmering before the fire."

Cinnamon toast served with cambric tea (a light tea, served with lots of milk and a little sugar) is ideal for children's tea parties—complete with dolls, toy dishes, an occasional dog or cat who will sit still at the child's tea table, and a patient adult who will use the opportunity to amuse, nurture, and just enjoy a small child on a rainy, cold, stay-at-home afternoon.

To make cinnamon toast, sprinkle several pieces of hot buttered toast with cinnamon and sugar. Usually the slices are trimmed and simply cut into triangles. For a special touch, use cookie cutters to cut the toast into animal or fancy shapes.

A PROPER POT OF TEA

When it comes to tea, we have three different categories to choose from: English tea, fruit tea, and herbal tea. Of the English teas, the light Earl Grey is my personal favorite. English breakfast tea is a heavy but popular tea. And for a truly heady flavor, which on occasion I love, try Lapsang souchong tea.

Tea tastes best prepared in a pot rather than in an individual cup. Heat the pot first by pouring boiling water into it, then pouring it out. Add one teaspoon of tea per cup to the warmed pot. (If you don't have loose tea, use tea bags.) Pour boiling water over the tea leaves and let the tea steep for five minutes. Then serve, using a hand strainer placed over the cup as you pour. If you use milk, add the milk to the teacup first; then pour the tea into the cup. A tea cozy, which fits over the pot, helps to keep the tea hot. Tea cozies can be handmade, or you can find them in a British import store or in some of the specialty catalogs that now come through the mail.

Having tea provides a ceremony of brewing, pouring, sipping, and conversing. In *The London Ritz Book of Afternoon Tea* by Helen Simpson it is said that

> Anna, 7th Duchess of Bedford, grew tired of the sinking feeling every afternoon around about 4 o'clock, in the long dull space of time between meals. In 1840 she plucked up courage and asked for a tray of tea, bread and butter, and cake to be brought to her room. Once she had formed the habit she found she could not break it, so spread it among her friends instead. As the century progressed, afternoon tea became increasingly elaborate.

Even today, continues Simpson,

> Whenever anything momentous occurs, whether matter for celebration or tragedy, a pot of tea is produced. When friends meet unexpectedly, they exchange news over tea.[4]

The definition of a proper tea varies from person to person. Generally, however, there are two ways of taking tea: afternoon tea and high tea. Those who stereotype all teas with delicate food and idle chatter are thinking of afternoon tea, which is, in truth, strictly a social event. Afternoon tea is properly served between the hours of 2:00 and 4:00.

Afternoon tea consists of light teas, finger sandwiches, and something sweet served on delicate china. The tea may be of the light, more traditional English type, such as Earl Grey, or it may be one of the many fruit teas or herbal teas that are available today. The sweet may be scones served with jam and Devonshire cream (see index), individual cakes, or a plain cake like Seedcake, a sweet that has been enjoyed since the Middle Ages. Because of the lightness of afternoon tea, most people still eat a regular evening meal later on. Afternoon tea assuages the mid-afternoon sugar drop many of us feel.

In contrast to afternoon tea, high tea is more of a meal and thus is served later, usually between 5:00 and 7:00 in the evening. While afternoon tea is considered a luxury or an exceptional pleasure, high tea provides more nutrition and becomes a heavier meal. Full sandwiches with chicken, tuna, and other more hearty fillings, along with a hot dish, replace the more delicate sandwiches of afternoon tea.

Finger Sandwiches •
204–205

Individual Frosted Cakes • 161

Seedcake • 135

Whereas delicate china and fancy dress characterize the social appeal of afternoon tea, less extravagant serving pieces and business attire often characterize a high tea. Both teas and kaffebords can, of course, be modified to serve different people's needs, but these are the primary guidelines associated with these occasions. The end result of serving coffee or tea, and of offering hospitality to one's family or to those who seek refuge at our hearth, is comfort and refurbishment.

Whether in joy or in crisis, the English turn to tea and the Swedes turn to coffee. Like many people, I'm so mixed into several cultures that I can turn to either.

HOSPITALITY PROVIDES LASTING MEMORIES

Long after my parents had died, an elderly neighbor said to me: "Your parents always thought of such nice things to do. Once when I was cleaning the porch in order to start painting, I was tired, hot, dusty, and hungry. It was noontime, but I didn't want to go inside and make lunch because I didn't want to take the time to clean up. Suddenly I turned around and there was your father with a plate of tasty sandwiches."

She continued, "On another occasion, when I had been injured in a car accident and had just gotten home from the hospital, we were having a heat wave. I was in pain and hot and miserable. That time your mother brought over a pitcher of the most delicious icy lemonade I've ever had. I'll never forget them," she concluded nostalgically.

I'm sure the sandwiches were just sandwiches, and certainly the lemonade was nothing out of the ordinary. But the timing and the love that went with the actions made them memorable in this woman's mind some twenty-five or thirty years later. This was hospitality.

To turn one's home into a welcoming hearth is to provide a place of safety for oneself, one's family, one's friends, and for the stranger at the door—and sometimes outside the door! Such a home becomes a place of hospitality out of which emanate love and caring.

Sometimes concepts become most clear through contrast. In *Saint Croix Notes* by Noah Adams, according to a review in the *Los Angeles Times:*

> On a chilly October morning, he reflects on the few inches of brick and plaster that protect him from the hostile elements, concluding, "On Halloween, if you are whimsical enough, you could think of trick-or-treaters as creatures out there in the dark, goblins surely, and wolves and bears. And we stay huddled inside the shelter, throwing out scraps of food and candy to appease them."[5]

Compare this with the words from the *Book of Common Prayer*—a prayer one might truly offer at the end of any act of hospitality:

> Send us now into the world in peace,
> and grant us strength and courage
> to serve and love you
> with gladness and singleness of heart;
> through Christ our Lord. Amen.

R·E·C·I·P·E·S

Cheese Straws

3 cups flour
2 teaspoons baking powder
1/2 teaspoon sea salt
1/4 teaspoon ground red pepper (cayenne)
3/4 cup freshly grated Parmesan cheese
1 1/4 cups grated cheddar cheese
1/2 cup butter
2 egg yolks, beaten
3 tablespoons cold water

Cheese straws have been served at White House functions since a recipe was provided in the 1887 edition of *The White House Cookbook.* Since that time, the recipe has changed some. The recipe included here is my own and is different from any of the others I have seen; it is unique and elegant.

1. In a large mixing bowl, sift together flour, baking powder, salt, and pepper. Stir in both cheeses. Then cut in butter with a pastry cutter or dull knife. Using your hands, mix into a paste, gradually adding the beaten egg yolks and water. The mixture should barely hold together.

2. On a slightly floured board, roll out the dough to a thickness of 1/3". (This dough is difficult to hold together and will need to be pinched at places where it splits apart.) With a sharp knife, cut the dough into 3" x 1 1/2" sticks. Place the sticks on an ungreased baking sheet, and bake in a preheated oven at 325° for about 10 minutes or until golden brown. Cool on wire racks and "Serve cold, piled tastefully on a glass dish."[1] Cheese straws can be served with hot soup, with a tossed green salad, or as an hors d'oeuvre.

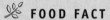
Ham Puffs

8 oz. cream cheese, softened
yolk of 1 hard-boiled egg, chopped
1 teaspoon baking powder
dash of sea salt
10–12 thin slices white sandwich bread
mayonnaise
4 1/2 oz. can deviled ham
paprika

1. Combine cream cheese with egg yolk, baking powder, and salt. Mix until blended and smooth. Using a biscuit cutter, cut about 4 small rounds from each slice of the bread. Spread each round lightly with mayonnaise and a thin layer of deviled ham. Spoon the cheese mixture over the ham and sprinkle with paprika. (This much can be done ahead and the appetizers can be frozen, if you wish.)

2. To serve (whether fresh or frozen), bake in a moderately hot oven (375°) for 12–15 minutes, or until puffed and browned. Serve immediately. Makes about 45 appetizers.

Julie's Authentic Salsa

1 dozen tomatoes (fresh)
4 yellow chiles (fresh)
4 jalapeno chiles (fresh)
4 serrano chiles (fresh)
(choice of chiles and amount used can be varied by taste)
1 bunch cilantro (chopped)
2 whole onions (chopped)
4 garlic cloves (freshly minced)
1/2 lemon (freshly squeezed)
salt and pepper (season to taste)

Create party magic with this familiar cultural standby.

This makes about 3 quarts, enough for any party, and refrigerate the rest! For smaller quantities, cut the amount of tomatoes, chiles, onions, cilantro, and garlic in half. For a milder-tasting salsa, cut the amount of chiles in half.

1. Roast tomatoes and chiles over the stovetop by holding them over a flame with tongs, or roast tomatoes and chiles over a barbecue grill. If you wish, you can also broil them in a conventional oven. Keep turning them until the skin is blackened on all sides. (Be sure to avoid getting face, hair, or hands too close to the fire and do not leave unattended.) As long as they are hot, touch only by the use of long tongs. Rinse off any remaining pieces of black skin.

2. Place the tomatoes and chiles between a moistened towel for five minutes; this will make it easier to peel the skin. Cut off stems and cut the chiles in half so that you can clean out the insides, but leave some seeds for flavor and taste. Dice all the tomatoes and chiles into fairly small pieces.

3. Rinse the cilantro and cut most of the stems off. Dice cilantro and onion. Mince four large cloves of garlic. Add lemon juice and minced garlic to salsa. Salt and pepper to taste. Refrigerate.

This **Authentic Salsa** is good with chips, fresh vegetables, nachos, tacos, enchiladas, salads, rice and beans, chicken, steak, and fish dishes.

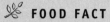

FOOD FACT

Avocados are high in fat and calories, but the fat is basically unsaturated and thus does not raise cholesterol levels. Avocados are also a good source of long-lasting protein.

Delicious Guacamole

4 avocados, peeled, chopped, or smashed

1 cup Authentic Salsa

Mix and serve with chips or with sour cream on nachos, tacos, enchiladas, or rice and beans

---

HELPFUL HINT

After you have prepared the guacamole, place avocado pit inside the mixture to keep the guacamole fresh and to prevent it from turning black.

Julie's Easy Homemade Salsa in 10 Minutes

2 28-ounce cans whole tomatoes

4 yellow chiles

2 jalapeno chiles (fresh)

2 serrano chiles (fresh)

(choice and amount of chiles can be varied by taste)

1 bunch cilantro

1 whole onion (chopped)

4 garlic cloves (minced)

1/2 lemon (freshly squeezed)

salt and pepper (season to taste)

Boil chiles for 5 to 10 minutes and clean as in Julie's Authentic Salsa. Add tomatoes, chiles, onion, and cilantro into blender until chopped—about 15 seconds. Add minced garlic and salt and pepper.

Voilà! Refrigerate!

Nutty Pumpkin Bread

This pumpkin bread freezes very well, and because of the use of oil in the recipe, rather than butter or margarine, the bread is very moist. Sometimes I make one large loaf for my own entertaining, plus four individual loaves, to use for gifts at Christmas. This year at Thanksgiving, I used this recipe to make muffins. I now like the muffins even more than the bread.

3 1/2 cups sifted flour	1 cup oil
2 teaspoons baking soda	4 eggs, beaten
1 1/2 teaspoons salt	2/3 cup water
1 teaspoon cinnamon	2 cups pumpkin
1 teaspoon nutmeg	1/2 cup chopped walnuts
3 cups sugar	poppy seeds, if desired

Sift together dry ingredients into mixing bowl. Make a well in the dry ingredients. Mix remaining ingredients together and pour into the well. Mix together until smooth. Apportion batter into desired number of loaf or muffin pans. Bake 1 hour at 350°.

🌿 FOOD FACT

Pumpkin in itself is a comfort food. It was one of the first vegetables to be cultivated by the American Indians, who used it in soups, stews, and breads. For all our lives, most of us have associated pumpkin pie and its spicy aroma with holidays and family and the hearth.

Rayne's Surprise Breakfast and Snack Puffs

2 eggs
1 cup plus 2 tablespoons milk
1 tablespoon butter, melted
1 1/2 cups flour
3 teaspoons baking powder
1/2 teaspoon salt
1 tablespoon cornmeal

1. Preheat oven to 350°. Beat eggs. Add milk and melted butter.

2. In a separate bowl, sift flour, salt, and baking powder. Add dry ingredients to the liquid, then beat only until mixed.

3. Pour mixture into heavily greased or non-stick muffin pan. Bake approximately 25 minutes or until golden and slightly puffed. To avoid having the puffs stick to the pan, remove them from the pan immediately.

Cut puffs open and add spreadable cheese, or butter and jam. You may think of your own filling or you may wish to offer a selection of different cheeses and jams from which your guests may choose to spread on their own puffs. Serve warm on an attractive plate.

Makes 10–12 servings.

Adults and children can enjoy the sweet taste as well as receiving the added benefit of some protein. Serve with a seasonal fruit, coffee, tea, or chocolate milk.

FOOD FACT

Cornmeal provides additional flavor and nutrition; but, above all, it adds a crunchy texture. Color, texture, and flavor are all important factors in any food preparation.

Seedcake

According to the late James Beard, one of the most noted cooks and cookbook writers of our time: "No tea table, in my opinion, is complete without a good seedcake. We nursed one all the time. It was always there, diminishing, until a brand-new one replaced it. When it was too stale, it was sometimes served toasted and buttered." This is his recipe. (Seedcake would also be good on a kaffebord table.)

1 cup butter
2 cups flour
5 eggs
1 cup sugar
1/2 teaspoon salt
1 teaspoon baking powder
1 teaspoon vanilla
1 to 2 tablespoons caraway seeds

> *"No tea table, in my opinion, is complete without a good seedcake."* —JAMES BEARD

1. Cream together the butter and flour. Add eggs, one at a time, beating the mixture thoroughly after each addition. Add sugar, salt, baking powder, vanilla, and caraway seeds. Beat for 4 or 5 minutes by hand, or 2 minutes with an electric mixer.

2. Butter and flour a 9" tube pan and pour the batter into this. Bake at 350° for one hour or until the cake tests done with a straw.[2]

Scones

2 cups flour
1/2 teaspoon soda
1/2 teaspoon cream of tartar
1/2 teaspoon salt
2 tablespoons chilled butter
3/4 to 1 cup buttermilk
1/4 cup currants, if desired
Cornmeal

1. In a large mixing bowl, sift flour with soda, cream of tartar, and salt. Cut the butter into the mixture with a pastry blender or two knives until the texture is coarse, not well blended. With a wooden spoon, stir in currants, if desired, and enough buttermilk to form soft dough.

2. Turn the dough onto a well-floured pastry board. Sprinkle lightly with flour. Knead (see page 143) dough for about two minutes. Divide the dough in half, and shape each half into a ball. Roll each ball to a thickness of 1/4". Cut like a pie into 4 wedges.

3. Sprinkle the baking sheet with cornmeal. Place scones on sheet about an inch apart. Bake at 475° for 15–20 minutes until golden brown. Makes 8 scones.

☀ HELPFUL HINT

Scones are traditionally served with plenty of butter and a variety of jams. A very tasty addition is Devonshire Cream. This can be made ahead of time and is best slathered on the scones after they have been buttered, either before or after the addition of jam, or by itself.

Mock Devonshire Cream

3–oz. package of cream cheese, at room temperature
1/4 cup sour cream
3 tablespoons confectioners' sugar
1/4 cup whipping cream

1. Combine cream cheese with sour cream and beat until light. Add confectioners' sugar and cream, and blend well. Cover and refrigerate for at least 1 hour.

2. Before serving, remove from refrigerator and allow the mixture
    to come to room temperature. Serve with scones. Makes about 2
    cups.

✒ FOOD FACT

Fat contributes significantly to our enjoyment of food. But its use
must be strictly limited in order to preserve health. It should be used
and enjoyed unashamedly on certain occasions. An understanding of
often-used but rarely explained terms will help in its judicial use. A
calorie is a unit of measurement of the amount of heat and energy sup-
plied by food after it is utilized by the body. *Cholesterol* is a fatty substance produced by the body. The body makes its own cholesterol in
adequate amounts for its needs. Certain foods, however, also supply
cholesterol: egg yolks, organ meats, nuts, and dairy products, for example. *Saturated fats* come from animals as well as from coconut palm
and palm kernel oil. Saturated fats are *not* cholesterol, but they help
raise cholesterol levels. *Unsaturated fats*, on the other hand, come
from plants and are preferable.

It is wise to make automatic changes in eating habits where the
change could be significant to your health but will not change your
enjoyment of food that much. For example, one cup of **whole milk** contains 33 mg. of cholesterol, whereas one cup of **nonfat milk** contains
only 4 mg. If you are substituting one cup of nonfat milk for one cup
of whole milk in a recipe, add a tablespoon of unsaturated oil.

Keep in mind that **fat, saturated or unsaturated**, has twice the
calories as the same amount by weight of protein or carbohydrates. Yet
total denial of fat can cause a sense of deprivation that can lead to
bingeing. Cheddar cheese is high in saturated fat, but eating just a
taste of that cheese or changing to a lower-fat form of the cheese are
two options.

BREADS, YEAST

Betty's Sweet Yeast Dough

This dough can be used in various combinations. For example, you could use one-third of the dough for rolls and make a coffee cake with the remaining two-thirds.

1 cup milk, scalded (heated just to the point of boiling)

1/2 cup butter, cubed

1/2 cup sugar

2 eggs, well beaten

1 teaspoon salt

2 packages active dry yeast

1/4 cup warm water

4 1/2 cups all-purpose flour (approximately)

8–10 pods cardamom, mashed, and/or 1 teaspoon lemon rind. (If using ground cardamom, 2 tablespoons.)

*Proof yeast (see **Helpful Hint** on p. 140) in the 1/4 cup of warm water.*

1. Pour hot milk over butter, sugar, and salt. Mix. Cool milk mixture, add proofed yeast and well-beaten eggs. Beat in flour to form a soft dough. Mix in cardamom and/or grated lemon rind. Knead until smooth; form into a ball. Put in bowl, cover, and allow mixture to rise until doubled.

2. The time needed for rising will vary according to conditions, such as weather. Do not place the dough near a draft, but if possible, place in a warm area. Bread can rise in cold weather, or in a cold location, but it will take much longer.

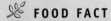 **FOOD FACT**

Cardamom is a plant found in Southern India. Its seeds, when dried, can be used as a spice. This spice is used extensively in the East and in Scandinavia where it is particularly popular in baked goods. Cardamom enhances flavor.

To Make Swedish Coffee Cake:

1. Punch the dough down and knead briefly. Place the dough on a greased cookie sheet or jelly-roll pan. Flatten into a long oval shape. Scatter 5 or 6 teaspoon-sized slices of butter across the dough. Sprinkle the dough generously with cinnamon and sugar. Add raisins or currants if desired. Fold the dough over once lengthwise.

2. Pinch the three sides tightly together at the very edges. Add more butter slices and then sprinkle more sugar and cinnamon across the top. Place several maraschino cherries on top of coffee cake for decoration. Now let the dough rise again until it is nearly doubled. Bake in preheated oven at 375° for 25–30 minutes.

To Make Crescent Dinner Rolls:

1. Divide the dough into three pieces. Roll each piece into a circle about 1/4" thick. Cut like a pie into six slices. Starting at the wide end, roll each slice. (If the ends come loose, pinch them together with a few drops of water to make them stick.)

2. Place the rolls on a pan. Allow the rolls to rise until double. Bake in a preheated oven at 375° for 25–30 minutes, or until the rolls are light brown in color.

   The rolls can be served plain or may be iced while they are still warm with an icing made from confectioners' sugar and water mixed together into a paste-like consistency.

To Make Cinnamon or Orange Rolls:

1. Divide the basic dough in half, rolling it out and spreading it with butter, cinnamon, sugar, and nuts; or sugar and grated orange rind mixed with a touch of juice.

2. Then roll the dough tightly and slice into individual rolls. Bake on a cookie sheet. You may also think of your own combinations.

⚜ HELPFUL HINT

Proofing yeast ensures that the yeast about to be used is fresh and active and will, in fact, cause the dough to rise. Yeast bread and coffee cakes are easy to make if a few simple rules are followed, and the results are so gratifying.

To proof yeast, mix the yeast into 1/4 to 1/2 cup warm water. Add 2 teaspoons of sugar to activate the yeast. (Salt slows down the rising activity.) In a short time the yeast will expand and bubble, beginning to ferment. It is then ready to be added to the dough as directed in the recipe. If there is no bubbling (fermentation) throw the mixture away and use a fresh supply of yeast.

Don't expect bread to rise normally in a draft. Ignore the clock and let the bread rise in its own time. It will rise faster in warm weather than in cold, for example. It can, however, rise in a refrigerator! Just count on an overnight process. Under the best of conditions the time will vary somewhat.

Kneading the dough evenly distributes the fermenting yeast and thus helps the bread rise. To knead, push down on the dough in one or two movements with both hands until it is flattened out. Then fold the dough over. Repeat the process for about six minutes *or* until the dough is smooth and shiny and bounces back after an indentation is made with a finger.

Kneading dough is an effective way to work out frustrations. Baking days are my back-to-earth days. They are, for me, a safety zone of simplicity and quick gratification.

Double Cheese Bread

Follow general operating directions for your specific bread machine. (This recipe is for a bread machine that makes 1 1/2–pound loaves.)

1. Add to the bread pan:

    3 cups bread flour
    1 1/2 tablespoons sugar
    1 1/2 tablespoons dry milk
    1 1/2 teaspoons sea salt
    1 1/4 cup water
    1 1/2 tablespoons butter
    3/4 cup grated cheddar cheese
    1/4 cup freshly grated Parmesan cheese
    1/4 cup cornmeal
    1/2 teaspoon Tabasco sauce

2. Close door of bread maker and add 3 teaspoons of active dry yeast to the yeast dispenser.

Monkey Bread

Monkey bread freezes well but is also delicious when served warm out of the oven. To serve, put the bread intact on an attractive plate and encourage your guests to pull pieces of bread off rather than trying to cut it. The butter into which the pieces have been dipped causes pieces of the bread to come apart quite easily. This bread is particularly good when served hot with jam.

1 cup milk
1 cup butter
1 teaspoon sea salt
2 packages yeast
1/4 cup warm water
1/4 cup sugar
3 eggs, beaten
4 1/2 cups flour (approximately)

1. In a small dish combine yeast and 1 tablespoon of sugar with warm water and allow to proof. (*See* note on proofing yeast, page 140.) Scald milk, being careful not to allow the milk to come to a boil. Add 1/2 cup of the butter, the remaining sugar, and the salt. Pour mixture into large mixing bowl and allow it to cool to lukewarm. Stir in beaten eggs and then the proofed yeast and mix well. Gradually beat in flour with a wooden spoon until you have a soft dough.

2. Turn the dough onto a floured board, adding flour as needed to avoid sticking. Knead the dough for approximately 10 minutes. (*See* note on how to knead, page 143.) Shape the dough into a ball, place it in a bowl, and cover with a dry towel. Let the dough rise in a warm, draft-free place until it is doubled in volume.

3. Once the dough has risen, punch it down several times while it is still in the bowl and wait for 5 minutes. Melt the remaining butter in a small saucepan. Then turn the dough onto a lightly floured board and shape into a ball. Divide the dough into two halves. Roll each portion out to a thickness of about 1/3". Using a sharp

knife, cut the dough into 3" diamond shapes. Dip each piece of dough, one by one, into the melted butter and layer the pieces in a 10" tube pan. The pan should be no more than half full.

4. Again, keeping the pan away from any draft, cover and let the dough rise until it is doubled. Bake in a preheated 375° oven until lightly brown (approximately 45 minutes). When you tap the top of the bread it should sound hollow. Let the bread cool for about 5 minutes in the pan before removing it.

Oatmeal Soy Bread

Follow general operating directions for your specific bread machine. (This recipe is for a bread machine that makes 1 1/2–pound loaves.)

1. Add to the bread pan:

2 1/2 cups bread flour	1 1/2 teaspoons sea salt
1/2 cup soy flour	3/4 cup water
1/4 cup oatmeal	1 1/2 tablespoons butter
1 1/2 tablespoons sugar	2 tablespoons poppy seeds
1 1/2 tablespoons dry milk	3/4 cup strawberry yogurt

2. Close door of bread maker and add 3 teaspoons of active dry yeast to the yeast dispenser.

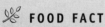

FOOD FACT

Poppy seeds are high in lecithin, which many feel is a powerful emulsifying agent, tending to break down cholesterol and fats in the blood. One characteristic of hardening of the arteries, or arteriosclerosis, is an increase in blood cholesterol and a decrease in lecithin. Some feel that lecithin may be an antidote for liver damage caused by drinking alcohol.

Soy Bread

Follow general operating directions for your specific bread machine. (This recipe is for a bread machine that makes 1 1/2–pound loaves.)

1. Add to the bread pan:

   2 3/4 cups bread flour
   1/2 cup soy flour
   2 tablespoons sugar
   1 1/2 tablespoons dry milk
   1 1/2 teaspoons sea salt
   1 1/4 cup water
   1/4 cup cornmeal
   1 tablespoon poppy seeds
   1 1/2 tablespoons butter

2. Close door of bread maker and add 3 teaspoons of active dry yeast to the yeast dispenser.

✻ HELPFUL HINT

An old baker's trick, dating back to the days when real live bakers made baked goods by hand from scratch, is to add grated lemon rind to the sugar before adding the sugar to the bread or coffee cake mixture. This brings out the various flavors in the baked goods.

The Erselius Family Eierkuchen

4 eggs, separated
3/4 cup milk
3/4 cup flour
1 teaspoon sugar
1/4 teaspoon sea salt
1/2 teaspoon baking powder

1. Beat the egg whites until stiff. In a separate bowl, beat the egg yolks along with the milk, sugar, and salt. Sift together the flour and baking powder and, with a wire whisk, gently mix with the egg yolk mixture. Lightly fold in the egg whites. Drop by tablespoonfuls on a hot, buttered skillet.

2. These pancakes should be a little larger than a silver dollar and can be served with butter and maple syrup, sour cream and syrup, fresh berries, or jelly. They taste particularly good with crisp bacon or little sausages. Makes about 20.

✂ FOOD FACT

If you are trying to limit your cholesterol by cutting down on **eggs**, remember that the high cholesterol level is found in the yolk. In recipes calling for eggs, you can substitute 3 egg whites for 2 whole eggs and 2 egg whites for one whole egg; or you can use one egg white plus 2 tsp. of unsaturated oil for each egg; or you can use commercial egg substitutes. Unless your doctor tells you differently, 3 eggs a week is a reasonable quota, providing good food value. Egg white is high in protein.

The Skoglund Family Swedish Pancakes

This recipe was a favorite of any guest who happened to share a meal of Swedish pancakes and bacon. They were served for special breakfasts, last-minute lunches, and Sunday evening suppers, as well as for a spur-of-the-moment meal if someone dropped by unexpectedly to share a problem or seek comfort of any kind. It was definitely comfort food.

2 eggs

2 cups milk

1 1/4 cups all-purpose flour (1/2 cup soy flour can be substituted for 1/4 cup of the all-purpose flour for added nutrition)

a pinch of salt

1/4 cup melted butter

a pinch of sugar

1. Beat the eggs. If desired, for added lightness, you can separate the eggs, add beaten yolks here, and then fold in beaten egg whites before pouring the mixture onto the skillet. Add milk and beat well. Gradually add flour, beating constantly. Add melted butter, salt, and sugar.

2. Pour approximately 1/3 cup batter onto a hot, buttered skillet to make a medium-size, crepe-like, thin pancake. Lightly brown on both sides and place the pancake on a plate that is kept warm by placing it on top of a pan half-full of simmering hot water. (This, by the way, is a good way to keep any kind of food warm while you are finishing the preparation of another food.)

   These pancakes can be served flat with a thin covering of maple syrup, but most Swedes prefer them covered with either syrup or cream and jam and then rolled up like a jelly roll and eaten.

CANDY

Nut Brittle

1 cup sugar
1/2 cup light corn syrup
dash of salt
3/4 cup each: shelled raw peanuts and pecans (Or use any
  1 1/2–cup combination of nuts. For peanut brittle use just
  peanuts.)
1 tablespoon butter
1 1/2 teaspoons baking soda
1 teaspoon vanilla

1. Combine sugar, corn syrup and salt in a 3–quart casserole. Stir in nuts.

2. Microwave at high (100%) until light brown (about 8–10 minutes), stirring once or twice.

3. Have remaining ingredients ready. Quickly stir them into the mixture until light in color and foamy. Quickly spread thin on a heavily greased baking sheet. Cool thoroughly, then break into pieces. Store tightly covered. Makes 1 lb. of candy.

CASSEROLES

Chicken Biscuit Casserole

    1/4 cup butter
    6 tablespoons flour
    1 cup milk
    1 cup chicken stock
    1/2 cup half-and-half
    1/3 cup celery, chopped
    3 tablespoons green pepper, chopped
    1 tablespoon chopped pimiento
    1 teaspoon salt
    1/4 teaspoon paprika
    2 cups diced, cooked chicken
    1/2 cup cooked rice

1. In a large saucepan melt butter. Add flour and mix into a paste. Gradually add milk, chicken stock, and half-and-half. Cook until creamy and slightly thickened.

2. In a small frying pan, lightly sauté celery and green pepper. Remove from heat, add pimiento; add mixture to the main saucepan. Mix in salt, paprika, chicken, and rice. Pour into a casserole dish large enough to allow room at the top for biscuits. Set aside and make biscuits.

Biscuits

    2 cups flour
    3 teaspoons baking powder
    1/2 teaspoon sea salt
    1/4 cup shortening
    3/4 cup milk

1. Sift the first three ingredients together in a mixing bowl. Cut in the shortening. Add milk and mix thoroughly.

2. Roll out the dough on a floured board or cloth until about 1/2" thick. With a cutter, cut into circles.

3. Arrange the biscuits on top of the casserole. Bake at 350° for 25 minutes or until biscuits are light brown.

Pork Sausage Casserole

1 lb. bulk pork sausage
1 chopped onion
1 green pepper, chopped
3 to 4 stalks of celery, chopped
salt and pepper to taste
1 cup uncooked, long-grain rice
4 cups chicken stock or chicken broth
1/2 cup thinly sliced almonds

1. Brown the pork sausage with the chopped onion. (Using freshly ground pork sausage, perhaps with sage, enhances the flavor and nutritional value of this dish.) Add chopped green pepper, chopped celery, and salt and pepper to taste.

2. Add uncooked, long-grain rice. Brown the mixture, stirring constantly.

3. Add chicken stock or chicken broth. Pour the mixture into a large casserole. Sprinkle almonds over the top. Bake at 350° for 1 hour.

Potato Casserole

8–10 medium potatoes
8 oz. cream cheese, softened
1/2 cup sour cream
4 tablespoons butter or margarine
salt and pepper to taste

1. Cook and mash potatoes. Add butter or margarine, salt, and pepper.

2. Cream softened cream cheese. Add sour cream and mix together until well blended. Add cream cheese mixture to mashed potatoes and whip until fluffy. A little more sour cream can be added if needed for better consistency.

3. Turn into a 2-quart casserole or into two 1-quart casserole dishes. Bake at 350° for 45–60 minutes, or until light brown on top. If you prefer, the potato mixture may be divided into individual foil potato boats and baked for approximately 30–45 minutes, or until light brown on top.

   This recipe can be frozen either in casserole form or divided into individual foil potato boats, which can be bought in the grocery store. It tastes better than mashed potatoes, and it is more elaborate than a baked potato.

Sweet Potato Puff

4 medium sweet potatoes
1/2 teaspoon grated nutmeg
1/4 teaspoon cinnamon
pinch of salt
1/4 teaspoon ground cloves
1/4 cup sugar
2 tablespoons butter
1 well-beaten egg

1/4 cup cream
1 1/2 tablespoons grated orange rind
1 tablespoon grated lemon rind
3 tablespoons light brown sugar
1/4 cup finely chopped walnuts or pecans (optional)

1. Cook the sweet potatoes in boiling water for 20 to 30 minutes, or until tender, covering the potatoes with water. Cool slightly. Peel the potatoes. The secret of the success of this recipe lies in the next step. After cutting the potatoes into several large pieces, put them into a mixer and beat until smooth. Continue to use the mixer as you add other ingredients.

2. Blend in the remaining ingredients one at a time, withholding 1 tablespoon of the butter and 2 tablespoons of the light brown sugar. Beat until fluffy.

3. Depending on the size of the potatoes, pour the mixture into a buttered 1- or 2-quart casserole. Melt the remaining butter and drizzle over the top of the mixture. Then sprinkle with brown sugar. You can also sprinkle some finely chopped walnuts or pecans over the top if desired.

4. Bake in preheated oven at 450° F. After five minutes, turn down to 400° F and bake for an additional 30 minutes or until brown.

DESSERTS

Kisses

Kisses were a major treat for me as a child. On very special Sundays, for very special guests, my mother would make fried chicken served with mashed potatoes and gravy, home-baked rolls topped with a sweet icing, pear halves stuffed with cream cheese, and—at the end—kisses. Kisses meant *special*.

> *Kisses were a major treat for me as a child. . . . Kisses meant special.*

The success of kisses depends upon ensuring that they are dry, not sticky. This is accomplished by allowing the kisses to remain in the oven for a sufficient time, as well as by carefully scooping them out. Humid weather can make this process more difficult. And, once again, pasteurized eggs are the safest.

4–5 egg whites (use pasteurized eggs*)
1 1/2 cups sugar
1/4 teaspoon sea salt
1 tablespoon vanilla

1. Beat egg whites and salt until they just hold a peak. Gradually add 3/4 cup sugar and continue beating for several minutes until very stiff. Fold in the last 3/4 cup of sugar along with the vanilla.

2. Drop the mixture by large spoonfuls onto a baking sheet lined with heavy waxed paper, making 10 or 11 kisses. Then go back and put a small spoonful on top of each kiss to form a cap.

3. Bake in a preheated oven at 250° for almost an hour, or until the kisses are light brown in color. Turn off the oven and allow the kisses to remain a little longer.

---

* See Food Fact on page 153.

4. After taking the kisses from the oven, remove them from the waxed paper. Gently loosen the caps; carefully scoop out and discard any soft portion that may remain in the center of the kisses.

Kisses can be filled with ice cream, whipped cream and berries, or any other desired filling. Place the cap on top of the filling. Frozen strawberries and whipped cream were the traditional filling in our family. For added attractiveness, serve each kiss on a paper doily placed on an attractive dessert plate.

 FOOD FACT

According to the Center for Disease Control and Prevention (CDC) egg-associated salmonella is an important health problem in the United States. Furthermore, salmonella is the number one cause of food poisoning in the U.S. Indeed it is estimated that one thousand people die from salmonella each year. In the past, egg-borne salmonella was the main problem. Then, in the 1970s strict procedures for egg cleaning and inspection were implemented, with excellent results. Now the greater danger is that salmonella enteritis infects the ovaries of hens and thus contaminates the eggs before the shells are formed. If the egg is thoroughly cooked, the salmonella organisms will be destroyed. Since most salmonella organisms live in the intestinal tracts of animals, including humans, hand washing after using the bathroom or after touching raw eggs, poultry, or meat is vital. Discard cracked or dirty eggs and keep eggs refrigerated.

In spite of these precautions, however, it is still dangerous to eat raw or partially cooked eggs, even as partially cooked as in a meringue. There are egg substitutes, but some of them do not work well with recipes like Snow Pudding (page 185). The safest approach by far is to use **pasteurized eggs**, just as most of us drink pasteurized milk, not raw milk.

continued on next page...

Davidson Eggs, produced by the Pasteurized Eggs Corporation, are becoming increasingly available. These eggs are treated by multiple warm water baths with no additives and are reportedly safe to eat, even raw if you so desire! More about Davidson Eggs can be learned by calling 800-410-7619 or going to their Web site at www.safeeggs.com. They will answer questions from the public. For more detailed information on salmonella there is also the CDC Web site at www.cdc.gov or call 404-639-2206.

Elizabeth's Old-Fashioned Popcorn Balls

4 quarts popped popcorn (unbuttered and plain)
1 cup sugar
1/3 cup molasses
1/3 cup water
1/4 cup butter
3/4 teaspoon salt
1 teaspoon vanilla

1. Place sugar, molasses, water, butter, and salt in a saucepan. Cook, stirring continually, until sugar is dissolved. Continue cooking without stirring until the mixture reaches 270° or until a small drop of the mixture forms a hard ball when added to cold water in a water glass. This process may take several different trials before you reach the hard ball stage. (Be sure to empty the glass of water after each test and fill it with fresh cold water before testing the mixture again.) Add the vanilla.

2. Divide the popcorn into two bowls. Working as quickly as possible, pour the syrup evenly over the popcorn in both bowls, mixing with a large spoon as you pour so that as much popcorn as possible is covered.

3. Being careful not to burn yourself on the hot syrup, and after

desserts

greasing your hands generously with butter, quickly shape handfuls of popcorn into about 12 medium-sized balls.

4. The popcorn balls should be cooled and then wrapped in waxed paper. To give them a festive look during a holiday like Christmas, wrap the waxed paper-covered balls in colored tissue paper and tie with ribbon. They make a colorful serving at each place setting on the table or tucked into a Christmas stocking or even heaped into a large bowl or basket.

The shelf life of popcorn balls wrapped in waxed paper should be approximately two weeks. If you want to freeze them, be sure that they are securely wrapped, first in waxed paper and then in a Ziploc bag or other airtight container. When defrosting, unwrap the ball completely to avoid making the popcorn soggy as it thaws.

While popcorn itself might not be tasty if frozen, the high heat to which the molasses is subjected seems to act as a preservative with these popcorn balls. In our test, a frozen popcorn ball that was defrosted after two months was as fresh and as enjoyable as when it was made.

✵ HELPFUL HINT

When freezing desserts in glasses, do not use your best crystal since there is always a chance of breakage. Berry Swirl (see page 67) provides a chance, however, to use color—bright red, deep blue, or forest green glasses—to accent your table setting. It is also a great way to use pretty wine glasses and fluted champagne glasses, whether or not you ever use them for wine or champagne.

CAKES

Aunt Esther's Coconut Layer Cake

2 cups sifted cake flour
2 teaspoons baking powder
1/2 teaspoon sea salt
2/3 cup butter, softened
1 cup sugar

3 eggs, separated
1/3 cup milk
1 teaspoon vanilla
1 small package shredded
   coconut

1. Sift flour once before measuring. Add baking powder and salt. Sift three times.

2. In another bowl, cream softened butter with a wooden spoon. Add sugar gradually, beating well after each addition until light and fluffy. Beat egg yolks until thick and add to the butter mixture. Beat once again until light and fluffy.

3. Add flour alternately with milk, a small amount at a time. Blend until smooth after each addition. Stir in vanilla and make sure the batter is well mixed—thick, smooth, and fluffy.

4. Beat egg whites until stiff, but not dry, and pile them lightly on top of batter. Fold gently into batter until the egg whites disappear. Work quickly in order to retain enclosed air, but do not overbeat.

5. Bake in two greased 9" layer pans at 375° for 25–30 minutes. Be careful not to overbake, since this cake dries out easily. Remove from oven and allow to cool in pans for 5 minutes. Remove from cake pans and cool on racks. (At this point the cake layers can be frozen for later use, if desired.)

6. Spread seven-minute frosting over cake and sprinkle with coconut and/or colored sprinkles.

Seven-Minute Frosting

> 2 egg whites, unbeaten
> 1 1/2 cups sugar
> 5 tablespoons water
> 1 1/2 teaspoons light corn syrup
> 1 teaspoon vanilla

1. Combine unbeaten egg whites, sugar, water, and corn syrup in top of double boiler. As you do this, beat the mixture continuously with a hand mixer until the mixture thickens and stands up in soft, snowy peaks when you lift the beater. With a good electric beater this will take approximately 12–15 minutes. Remove immediately from boiling water. Add vanilla and beat until the frosting will hold firm little ridges as it falls back from the beater. At this point it will be cool and thick enough to spread.

2. Brush off any crumbs from the cake layers. Frost lower layer, and place other layer on top. Frost sides of cake next, starting at the top, then pile the remaining frosting on the center top and spread out to edges. Swirl frosting into ridges with the back of a spoon. If you wish, chopped nuts, coconut, or a touch of food coloring can be folded into this frosting to provide variety. Colored sprinkles can also be scattered on top of the frosting to add a look of festivity.

Boston Cream Cake

Sometimes called Boston cream pie, this dessert goes way back in American history—the *New York Herald* first mentioned it in 1855. It was on the menu at the famous Parker House Hotel in Boston from the day it opened in 1856. It was at the Parker House Hotel that a version with chocolate frosting was developed. Earlier, it was filled with raspberry jelly and was called Mrs. Washington's pie. Obviously this recipe has many versions and many names, but its frequent appearance is eloquent testimony to its popularity. The following recipe is the version my mother used and handed down to me.

4 eggs, separated
1 cup sugar
4 tablespoons hot water
1 cup cake flour
1/2 teaspoon sea salt
1 teaspoon vanilla

In a large mixing bowl, beat the egg yolks with the sugar until thick and lemon-colored. Alternately, add water and sifted dry ingredients. Fold in the stiffly beaten egg whites and the vanilla. Pour into two round 8" buttered cake pans. Bake in preheated 350° oven for approximately 20 minutes.

Custard Filling
3 egg yolks, beaten
3 tablespoons all-purpose flour
3 tablespoons cornstarch
1/2 cup confectioners' sugar
2 cups whole milk (or extra rich)
2 tablespoons butter
1 cup whipping cream with vanilla to taste

1. In a double boiler combine all ingredients gradually, one by one, except whipping cream, stirring as you go. Cook until thick, stirring constantly. Cool to lukewarm. Fold in cream, whipped.

2. Carefully slice each cake layer into two layers so you have four layers. Brush off crumbs. Spread first three layers with custard filling. Place the four layers on top of each other leaving the top layer plain. Spread chocolate frosting over the top layer, allowing it to drip down over the sides of the cake.

Chocolate Frosting

1/2 cup brown sugar
1/2 cup water
2 tablespoons butter
2 squares unsweetened chocolate
2 cups confectioners' sugar
1 teaspoon vanilla
A pinch of salt

Combine brown sugar, water, and butter in a heavy saucepan and boil for 2 or 3 minutes. Add chocolate and stir. When the chocolate is melted remove the pan from the stove and add confectioners' sugar, vanilla, and salt. Beat until smooth. Immediately spread on the cake.

Candle Cakes

The following recipe is one of my mother's old standard recipes for cupcakes. It can be used also to make one or more candle cakes for a child's birthday (or even for an adult).

1/2 cup butter
1 cup sugar
4 eggs, well beaten
1 1/2 teaspoons baking powder
1 cup cake flour
1 teaspoon vanilla

1. In a medium-size mixing bowl, cream the butter and the sugar until they are light and fluffy. Add well-beaten eggs and beat until smooth. Gradually add sifted flour and baking powder. Add vanilla.

2. For best results, line muffin wells with paper baking cups. Fill each cup 3/4 full. If any baking wells remain empty, remove paper cup and fill to half-full with water. Bake in moderate oven (350°) until done. Cool. Remove from muffin tin.

3. For cupcakes, top with cupcake frosting and, if desired, decorate with coconut, colored sugar, or sprinkles. For a touch of elegance serve on a lace paper doily.

4. To make candle cakes, cover each cake entirely with seven-minute frosting (see recipe on page 157), or use the Cupcake Frosting listed below, and sprinkle thickly with shredded coconut. (The frosting can also be tinted with a tiny bit of food coloring.) Put a candle in the middle of each cake. Serve individually on plates or place on individual doilies on a large platter.

⚘ HELPFUL HINT

When freezing a cake always refrigerate it first. When possible, freeze the cake unfrosted; then frost the cake right before serving. When defrosting a cake, first remove all wrapping so that moisture does not collect and make the cake soggy.

Cupcake Frosting

1 teaspoon unflavored gelatin
2 tablespoons cold water
2 egg whites (use pasteurized eggs*)
1/2 cup sugar
1/2 teaspoon vanilla

1. Add gelatin to cold water and dissolve over hot water in double boiler.

2. In a separate bowl, beat the egg whites until stiff. Gradually add sugar to the egg whites, beating after each addition. Then add vanilla. Very slowly, add the dissolved gelatin to the egg white mixture, beating after each addition. Use pasteurized eggs.

---

* See Food Fact on page 153.

Ice Cream Cake Cones

This is another individualized cake idea, especially good for children in an outdoor celebration in the backyard or in a park, where a general mess will not be a problem.

1. Buy enough ice cream cones with flat bottoms to provide one for each child, plus a few extra. Fill the cones 3/4 full with cake batter. Put each cone into a cupcake well in a cupcake pan. Be sure to add a little water to any empty wells. Bake at 350° until a toothpick inserted into the middle of the batter comes out clean.

2. Transport the cones—along with ample amounts of ice cream and chocolate chips, chopped nuts, granola, small candies, and colored sprinkles—to the place of the party. Fill each cone with ice cream and then allow the children to decorate their own ice cream cake cones as they desire. Because you do this outside, spilled sprinkles and tipped over cones will not dampen the spirits of an otherwise fun time. The birthday person can have a candle to put in the top of the cone, so that he or she can make a wish and blow it out. These cones can also be used to celebrate an athletic victory or for any special occasion.

Individual Frosted Cakes

Small cakes, frosted in a variety of colors and shapes, enhance any tea table or kaffebord. Yet they can be made with less effort than it would seem. One basic recipe can make a variety of different-looking cakes. Individual cakes look particularly attractive when served on a tiered cake server.

> 1 2/3 cups sifted cake flour
> 1 1/2 teaspoons baking powder
> 1/3 cup butter
> 1 cup sugar

2 eggs, well beaten
1/2 cup milk
1 teaspoon vanilla

1. Measure sifted flour. Add baking powder and sift again. Cream butter, add sugar gradually, stirring all the time, and beat until light and fluffy. Thoroughly blend in eggs. Gradually stir in flour mixture, alternating the addition of flour with the milk, a small amount at a time. Add vanilla and mix thoroughly.

2. Using a cupcake pan, fill each cup 2/3 full. Or fill a square or oblong pan. Or use a cupcake pan and a small square pan, for a variety of shapes. Bake in moderate oven (375°) until a straw or toothpick inserted into one of the cakes comes out clean. Cover with any frosting desired.

Tinted Seven-Minute Frosting (page 159) looks good on small cakes. If a square or oblong pan is used, the cake may be cut into oblong wedges, triangles, and squares and then frosted with one or more colored frostings and topped with nuts, sprinkles, candies, or coconut.

When cutting a sheet cake into various shapes, be sure to brush off all the crumbs before frosting.

Jell-O Cake

I was brought up in a family with a no-cake-mixes, everything-made-from-scratch mentality. TV dinners were so rarely used that to me as a child they were actually a treat because they were different. In my late teens I went to a monthly Bible study where dinner was potluck. My friend always brought an angel food cake. Coming as I did from a family of excellent bakers, I knew how much was involved in making an angel food cake. A dozen eggs or so, for starters! My friend was famous for her cake, so I figured it had to come from an extra-special, long-cherished family recipe. Then one day she told me her secret. It was a cake mix. I have to admit I still loved it. I never again made an angel food cake from scratch.

One exception to my aversion to cake mixes is Jell-O cake. Jell-O cake is made from a mix, with other ingredients added to it. My mother made it for fairly ordinary occasions, and everyone always loved it. This is a moist cake and will keep well in the refrigerator.

1 package yellow cake mix
3–oz. package lemon gelatin
3/4 cup corn oil
3/4 cup cold water
grated lemon rind
4 eggs

1. In a large mixing bowl, mix the first five ingredients together. Add the eggs, one at a time, beating well after each addition.

2. Bake in a buttered and floured 9" x 13" pan in a 350° oven for 40 minutes. Remove from the oven. Cool slightly. With a fork, prick holes randomly across the top of the cake.

Topping

4 tablespoons lemon juice
1 1/3 cups confectioners' sugar

Mix these two ingredients together and spread over the cake as a glaze. Then put the cake into a paper bag and close the bag. When the cake is completely cool, it is ready to serve.

Nut Torte

> 3 1/4 cups chopped nuts (walnuts, black walnuts, or
> pecans work well)
> 6 tablespoons all-purpose flour
> 1 teaspoon baking powder
> 1/4 teaspoon sea salt
> 6 eggs, separated
> 1 cup sugar
> 1 teaspoon vanilla
> 1 cup whipping cream

1. Reserve 1 tablespoon of coarsely chopped nuts. Finely grind the remaining nuts. In a medium mixing bowl, combine the ground nuts, flour, baking powder, and salt. In a large mixing bowl, beat egg whites until they form soft peaks. In a small mixing bowl, beat egg yolks with sugar and vanilla until thick and lemon-colored. Gently fold first the nut mixture and then the yolk mixture into the beaten egg whites.

2. Preheat oven to 350°. Grease two 8"round cake pans, line the bottom of each pan with waxed paper, and grease the waxed paper. Pour batter into pans. Bake 25–30 minutes or until the top of the cake springs back when touched with finger. Cool the cake in the pans for 5 minutes. Remove from pans and cool on wire racks.

3. Beat cream until soft peaks form. Spread half of the whipped cream between the two layers. Spread the top of cake with remaining whipped cream. Sprinkle the remaining tablespoon of chopped nuts over the top of cake. Refrigerate the cake until serving time. Makes 12 servings.

Betty's Danish Cookies

Danish cookies were one of my mother's favorites for the Christmas season. Sometimes she made them for other special events, like a bridal shower or a tea.

> 2 cups sifted flour
> 1/4 teaspoon hartshorn salts (Ammonium carbonate, available at any drugstore—I buy it at a Swedish import store.)
> 3/4 cup butter
> 1/2 cup sugar
> 1 egg yolk

1. In a small mixing bowl sift the flour and hartshorn together and set aside. In a larger mixing bowl, cream the butter. Gradually add sugar to the butter, creaming until fluffy after each addition. Thoroughly blend in the egg yolk with the butter mixture. Gradually add the dry ingredients to the butter mixture, mixing thoroughly as added. Set aside.

2. Cut the dough into halves and set one half aside. Roll out the other half of the dough on a lightly floured board until it is 1/8" thick. Cut into diamond-shaped pieces with a cookie cutter. Place the cookies on a greased cookie sheet and lightly spread each cookie with the meringue. Repeat with the second half of the dough. Bake at 375° for 10 minutes or until lightly browned. After removing from the oven, leave the cookies on the cookie sheets for about 2 minutes. Using a spatula, carefully remove the cookies onto wire racks until cool. Makes about 6 dozen cookies.

Meringue

1 egg white (use pasteruized eggs*)
1/8 teaspoon salt
1 1/4 cups sifted confectioners' sugar

Beat the egg white and salt until frothy. Beating well, gradually add the sifted confectioners' sugar. Continue beating until rounded peaks are formed.

Betty's Swedish Pepparkakor

Pepparkakor are the most traditional of all Swedish Christmas cookies. The fragrance of these cookies, and their attractive appearance, make them a vital part of the Christmas celebration. Each family, or at least each village, in Sweden seems to have its own version of this recipe. This was my mother's, and perhaps my maternal grandmother's.

1 cup butter	1 tablespoon warm water
1 1/2 cups sugar	3 cups sifted flour
1 egg, beaten	3 teaspoons cinnamon
1 teaspoon dark corn syrup	2 teaspoons ginger
2 teaspoons soda	1 teaspoon cloves

1. In a large bowl cream the butter. Beating continually, gradually add sugar. Beat in the egg and corn syrup. Dissolve the soda in the warm water and add to the butter mixture. Mix well. Sift the remaining dry ingredients together. Gradually add the dry ingredients to the butter mixture. Mix well. Chill for several hours.

2. Take a small portion of the dough and roll it out until very thin on a lightly floured board. Cut cookies with a floured cookie cutter and place on a greased cookie sheet. The cookies can be decorated very simply with a small piece of almond placed in the center. Or they can be sprinkled with various colored sugars.

---

* See Food Fact on page 153.

3. Bake at 400° for 6–8 minutes, or until done. Place on wire racks to cool and store in tightly sealed tins. Yields approximately 4 dozen medium-size cookies.

Bonbon Cookies

Bonbon cookies stand out on any cookie platter and add a touch of color to the general decorations. These are wonderful for bridal or baby showers, as well as for Christmas.

1/2 lb. butter
1/3 cup sifted confectioners' sugar
3/4 cup cornstarch
1 cup sifted flour

In a large mixing bowl cream softened butter. Sift and thoroughly mix the dry ingredients. Gradually add the dry ingredients to the butter and thoroughly blend. Drop by small teaspoonfuls onto ungreased cookie sheet. Bake at 350° for 10–12 minutes or until slightly brown.

Frosting

1 small package cream cheese
1 cup confectioners' sugar
1 teaspoon vanilla

Thoroughly blend cream cheese, confectioners' sugar, and vanilla. Divide the mixture into two small bowls. Add a few drops of green food coloring to the first mixture and red food coloring to the second mixture. Blend well. Frost half of the cookies with the green frosting and half with the red frosting. These should look like bonbon candies.

Cream Wafers

Cream wafers are impressive and tasty. These cookies are also very versatile and can be used for a variety of special occasions.

1 cup softened butter
2 cups flour
1/3 cup whipping cream

1. Cream and mix all the ingredients together and chill.

2. Working with one-third of the dough at a time, roll out the dough on a floured board until 1/8" thick. Cut out rounds with a cookie cutter. Transfer the rounds to a piece of waxed paper heavily coated with granulated sugar. Coat both sides. Transfer the rounds to an ungreased cookie sheet. Prick each round with a fork three or four times. Bake for about 7 minutes at 350°.

3. To make each cream wafer, put two cookies together with the filling between them. Store in refrigerator. These cookies should be used within a few days of making them. If you wish to make them earlier, you can freeze the cookies before adding the filling.

Filling

1/4 cup softened butter
1/4 cup confectioners' sugar
1 egg yolk (use pasteurized egg*)
1/4 teaspoon vanilla

In a separate bowl make a filling by combining and thoroughly mixing the softened butter, confectioners' sugar, egg yolk (use pasteurized egg), and vanilla.

---

* See Food Fact on page 153.

Dora's Shortbread

A year-round favorite at the Ken Connolly home, these cookies were meticulously cut into perfect pieces by Ken's mother, who had brought the recipe from Scotland. As the busy wife of a pastor, Dora Connolly still found time to make it in large quantities each Christmas and give it packed in tins to friends who eagerly looked forward to it.

> 1 cup butter (do not use margarine)
> 3/4 cup sugar
> 3 cups flour

1. Cream butter and sugar together in large bowl. Adding 1/2 cup at a time, mix in the flour with a wooden spoon to make a stiff dough. Roll out between sheets of waxed paper to a size of approximately 8" x 10", and 1/2" thick. Cut into pieces that are 1" x 2 1/2".

2. Place on cookie sheet. At a slight angle prick lengthwise with a fork. Sprinkle lightly with white sugar. Bake for about 50 minutes at 275°. The cookies should be just barely colored when done, but not brown. Remove to wire rack. Cool completely. Store in tightly covered container.

Gingerbread Boys

While many Christmas cookies originate in other countries and remind some of us of our heritage, the gingerbread boy is truly an American cookie and, as such, provides the basis for some American cookie memories.

Gingerbread boys make wonderful treats for children when they are individually wrapped in clear plastic. To personalize the cookies, decorate them as girls and/or boys and write the child's name on the cookie with frosting. The same gingerbread dough can also be used with any number of different cookie cutter shapes and then decorated.

4 cups flour   1 tablespoon ginger
   (approximately)   1/4 teaspoon cinnamon
1/2 lb. butter   1 teaspoon sea salt
1 cup sugar   dark molasses

1. Mix the flour, sugar, spices and salt together in a large mixing bowl. Cut in the butter with a knife or fingertips. Add just enough molasses to hold the ingredients together as you mix them with your fingers. Once the dough adheres, let it chill overnight in a covered dish.

2. Divide the dough into several pieces and roll out each one thinly on a floured board. Cut into gingerbread boys, using a cookie cutter. Place on a greased cookie sheet and decorate using raisins, currants, bits of nuts, and colored sugar. Bake in moderate oven (350°) until lightly brown. After they are baked, they can also be decorated with colored icing.

Gingerbread Christmas Tree Ornaments

This recipe makes a tougher cookie than is ordinarily used for Christmas cookies. Any shape cookie cutter can be used. Just be sure to put a small hole at the top of the cookie before baking, through which a narrow red or green ribbon can be tied. Leave enough space so that the ribbon or cord doesn't break through the top. With the use of colored frosting, these cookies can be decorated and even personalized by writing the name of a friend on the ornament. These make special gifts for children to give to their friends and family. And even though they are a little tough, they can be safely eaten.

1 cup shortening (do not use butter or margarine)
1 cup sugar
1 cup molasses
5 cups flour
1/2 teaspoon sea salt

3 teaspoons ginger
1 teaspoon soda
1 teaspoon nutmeg
1 teaspoon cinnamon

1. Mix together shortening, sugar, and molasses. Sift together the flour, sea salt, ginger, soda, nutmeg, and cinnamon. Using your hands, thoroughly mix all ingredients together.

2. On a floured surface, roll out the dough to a thickness of about 1/3″. Using your choice of cookie cutters cut out the dough and bake on a greased cookie sheet at 375° until lightly browned.

Grandma Erselius's Honey Kuchen

4 eggs
1 cup brown sugar
1/2 teaspoon cardamom
  (See note on page 139.)
1 cup honey
1 cup milk
1 cup chopped nuts

1/2 cup cut-up citron
grated rind of 1 lemon
1 teaspoon cloves
2 teaspoons cinnamon
1 teaspoon baking soda
1 teaspoon sea salt
3 1/2 cups all-purpose flour

1. In a large mixing bowl beat the eggs. Blend in the brown sugar. Blend in honey, then milk, mixing well each time. Sift together flour, cloves, cinnamon, baking soda and salt. Gradually add to the egg mixture, beating well after each addition. Add crushed cardamom, nuts, citron, and lemon rind until all ingredients are thoroughly mixed.

> ✳ **HELPFUL HINT**
>
> When measuring brown sugar, always pack it down in the measuring cup rather than filling it loosely as with flour or white sugar. Your measurement will then be accurate.

2. Pour into an ungreased sheet cake pan. Bake at 350° for approximately 25 minutes or until nicely browned.

3. Remove from the oven and immediately loosen from the pan with a spatula. Carefully trim the edges. Ice with an egg-white and confectioners' sugar icing, flavored with almond extract. After adding a thin icing, scatter colored sprinkles over the top. Cut into small cakes of about 1″ x 1 1/2″. "The older the better in a tin box."

Icing

1 egg white (use pasteruized eggs*)
1 1/4 cups sifted confectioners' sugar
1/4 teaspoon almond extract

Beat the egg white until stiff but not dry. Add the confectioners' sugar and almond extract and blend well. Add a few drops of water until the mixture is the right consistency for spreading.

Marilyn's Sugar Cookies

Like pepparkakor, recipes for sugar cookies seem to abound. Sugar cookies are very American. This recipe is one I obtained from my friend Marilyn.

1/2 lb. butter	*3 cups sifted flour*
2 cups sugar	*2 teaspoons baking powder*
2 eggs	*1/2 teaspoon sea salt*
2 teaspoons vanilla	*1/8 teaspoon cinnamon*

1. In a large mixing bowl cream butter. Gradually add sugar, beating until light and fluffy. Add eggs one at a time and mix thoroughly. Add vanilla. Sift dry ingredients together and gradually add to butter mixture, blending thoroughly. Chill dough.

2. Roll out on lightly floured board to 1/8″ thickness. Cut with a floured cookie cutter. Place on ungreased cookie sheet and

---

* See Food Fact on page 153.

either sprinkle with colored sugar before baking or frost after baking. Bake at 350° for about 12 minutes. Cool on racks and store in tightly sealed tins.

Mary's Speculatius

Speculatius is a white dough cutout cookie. This recipe came from Germany and was one of those many recipes that were handed across the backyard fence.

4 cups flour

2 cups sugar

1/2 lb. butter

2 eggs

1 teaspoon grated lemon rind

1 teaspoon cinnamon

1/4 teaspoon sea salt

1/8 teaspoon hartshorn salts (Ammonium carbonate, available at any drugstore—I buy it at a Swedish import store.)

1. In a large mixing bowl cream the butter, gradually adding the sugar until the two are totally mixed. Beat the eggs separately and add to the butter mixture, mixing thoroughly. Mix in the lemon rind. Sift together the flour, cinnamon, and salt and add gradually to the butter mixture. Mix in hartshorn salts.

2. On a floured board roll out the mixture until it is about 1/8" thick. If the dough is difficult to work with, refrigerate before rolling it out. Using cookie cutters, cut the dough into various shapes. Decorate as with other cut-out cookies. On an ungreased cookie sheet bake 10 to 12 minutes at 350° or until lightly brown. Remove while hot and allow to cool on wire racks. Store in tightly sealed tins to retain crispness.

Mexican Wedding Cakes

Alternately called Vienna kipfels, Mexican wedding cakes are delicious served by themselves or with other cookies. They add variety. Once when I was taking a graduate course at night, right before Christmas, I brought a large box of these cookies to share with the class. They were the hit of the season.

1 cup butter

1/2 cup sifted confectioners' sugar

1 teaspoon vanilla

2 1/4 cups sifted flour

1/4 teaspoon sea salt

3/4 cup finely chopped nuts (walnuts, pecans, or almonds)

1. In a large bowl mix the ingredients together in the order given and chill for about 3 hours.

2. Roll into small balls the size of walnuts or roll out the balls and shape them into crescents. Place on a greased cookie sheet. Bake in a slow oven (250°–300°) for about 45 minutes so that the balls are set but not brown. While still warm roll in confectioners' sugar. Cool and roll in confectioners' sugar again. Makes 4 dozen.

Molasses Sticks

These cookies were a favorite childhood treat, in addition to the more usual chocolate chip or oatmeal cookies. The recipe came over the fence from the kitchen of Mary Erselius. In later years she would sometimes make a box full of these cookies for my birthday.

1/2 cup sugar	1/2 teaspoon soda
1/2 cup dark molasses	1 teaspoon ginger
1/2 cup butter	2 1/2 cups flour

1. Using a medium-size saucepan, heat the first three ingredients together to boiling point. Remove immediately from stove. Add soda and ginger. After the mixture foams up, quickly add 2 cups flour and mix rapidly.

2. You will need the other half-cup of flour, or slightly more, while rolling the dough out on a pastry cloth or board. Divide the dough into two parts. Roll each part out into an oblong shape the size of a cookie sheet. Cut into strips approximately 1 1/8" wide and 6"–8" long.

3. Place each molasses stick on a lightly greased cookie sheet. Bake at 350° for 6–8 minutes. Remove from cookie sheet and allow to cool on racks. These cookies become crisp as they cool. In order to retain their crispness they need to be stored in a tightly sealed container.

Spritz Cookies

Spritz cookies are made by filling a cookie press, and have been a traditional Swedish cookie for generations. According to custom these cookies have been baked in an "S" shape or in a ring. For variety they can be made into a round cookie with a small depression made in the center to which jelly or 1/4 maraschino cherry may be added before baking. A particularly festive look can be achieved by sprinkling the unbaked cookies, of any shape, with green or red colored sugar. Another way to give this cookie a festive touch is to put a few drops of food coloring into the dough. Green and red, if not overdone, work well.

In any family, certain foods on certain occasions become associated with a specific family member. In our family, spritz cookies were usually made by my aunt Lydia, and so I associate them with her. Watching her make these cookies in various shapes and colors remains a memory she created for me as a child.

2 1/2 cups sifted flour   *1/2 cup sugar*
1 cup butter   *2 egg yolks*
1 teaspoon vanilla

1. In a large mixing bowl cream together the butter and vanilla extract. Add the sugar gradually, creaming until fluffy after each addition. Beat in egg yolks, one at a time, and blend thoroughly.

Add flour gradually and mix thoroughly as it is added.

2. Fill your cookie press about two-thirds full with dough. Use the manufacturer's directions to form cookies of various shapes onto a cookie sheet. Bake at 350° for 12–15 minutes, or until cookies are golden. Carefully remove the cookies with a spatula and place on cooling racks. Cool completely and store in tightly sealed tins to preserve crispness.

Betty's Apple Pie

(My mother gave this recipe to my daughter, Rayne)

Crust

This piecrust can be used with many different fillings. For one double crust (or two single crust pie shells):

3 cups all-purpose flour   1 teaspoon sea salt
1 cup shortening   6 tablespoons cold water

1. Sift the flour and salt together. Cut shortening into flour with dough blender or spatula. Sprinkle cold water, 1 tablespoon at a time, over the mixture. Lightly mix until dough is formed. Divide into two balls. Wrap tightly and refrigerate until chilled.

2. Roll each ball to desired thickness, about 1/8". Fit bottom piecrust into 9" pie plate, making sure that the edges extend slightly over the top. Make filling.

Filling

7–9 medium apples, peeled,   1 teaspoon flour
   cored, and sliced   1 tablespoon sugar
3/4 cup sugar (adjust   1/2 teaspoon cinnamon
   according to tartness   1 tablespoon butter
   of apples)

1. Combine flour with 3/4 sugar and sprinkle mixture over bottom of pie shell. Fill with sliced apples. Cover with remaining sugar and cinnamon. Dot with butter, cut into several pieces. Moisten the edge of the pie with water. Fit the top crust over apples, seal edge of pie, and flute with fork.

2. Bake at 350° for 40 minutes, or until crust is brown and apples are tender.

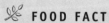
Lemon Fluff Pie

6 eggs, separated (use pasteurized eggs*)
juice from 1 1/2 lemons
rind of 1 lemon, grated
3 tablespoons boiling water
1/8 teaspoon sea salt

1 cup confectioners' sugar
6 tablespoons granulated sugar
1 baked pie shell (see recipe on page 179)

Beat egg yolks until lemon-colored. Add juice and rind of lemon, water, salt, and confectioners' sugar. Cook in a double boiler until thick. Cool. Fold in 3 of the egg whites, stiffly beaten.

Meringue

3 egg whites (use pasteurized eggs*)
6 tablespoons granulated sugar

1. In a separate bowl, beat the remaining 3 egg whites until frothy. Gradually add the sugar, beating until stiff.

2. Fill the baked pie shell with the lemon mixture. Cover with meringue. Bake in hot oven (450°) until meringue is lightly browned. Watch closely.

---

* See Food Fact on page 153.

Creamy Pumpkin Pie

2 cups of pumpkin puree
2 tablespoons flour
2 eggs
2 1/2 cups whole milk
3/4 cup sugar

1/2 tablespoon ground ginger
1/2 tablespoon ground
   cinnamon
1/4 teaspoon nutmeg
pinch of salt

1. Using a mixer and adding each ingredient one at a time, mix all of the ingredients until smooth and pour into baked crust. (See pastry recipe below.)

2. Bake at 350° until pie surface is smooth and fork comes out clean when inserted into the center of the pie (approximately 1 hour plus).

   Refrigerate pie before serving. Serve with whipped cream or ice cream. Garnish as desired (i.e., chocolate curls or fresh mint leaves).

Plain Pastry for One-Crust Pie

2 cups of all-purpose flour
1/2 teaspoon salt
1/4 cup diced butter
3 tablespoons shortening (Crisco)
3 tablespoons ice water

1. Mix salt with flour. Work in butter and shortening with fingertips, fork, or pastry blender until shortening is evenly mixed in bits no larger than peas. Using a cutting motion with the fork, add water and work the mixture with your fingers until the dough adheres together slightly. With your hands, form the mixture gently into a ball. Wrap in waxed paper and chill (about 1 hour).

2. On a floured board, roll the mixture out to approximately 1/8-inch thickness and place dough into a 9-inch round pan. Trim edges. Weight the bottom of the pie crust with pie weights or even dried beans before baking. Bake at 350° F for five minutes.

PUDDINGS

Puddings make wonderful desserts for children and for adults. They also make good comfort food and are excellent fare for those who are sick or convalescing. Remember, some of these recipes contain raw eggs. (See Food Fact on page 153.)

Baked Custard

Baked custard is simple enough for a child to make. As a matter of fact, it is an excellent recipe to use in teaching children how to cook. Baked custard, topped with whipped cream, can be an excellent simple dessert. It is also particularly good for offering simple-to-eat nutrition during an illness or convalescence. In my own childhood memory bank, baked custard stands out both as a dessert served after a light Sunday night supper and, particularly, as one of the first foods you could eat and enjoy after being sick.

> *4 cups scalded milk*
> *4 eggs*
> *pinch of salt*
> *1/2 cup sugar*
> *nutmeg, as desired*

1. In a medium-size bowl, combine the eggs and salt and beat lightly. Gradually add the sugar, beating constantly, and slowly add the scalded milk. Pour into buttered custard cups, which are then placed in a shallow pan with a small amount of water (1"–2"). Sprinkle ground nutmeg over each cup of custard and bake in a slow oven until firm.

2. To test the custard, insert a clean silver knife gently into the center of the custard. When the knife comes out perfectly clean, the custard is done. Do not overcook or the custard will curdle.

   If desired, low-fat milk may be substituted for whole milk.

Betty's Rice Pudding

This particular pudding has been in our family for as long as I can remember. It is a traditional dish on Christmas Eve as well as a light supper dish for Sunday evening.

2 cups milk
1/3 cup sugar
4 eggs, slightly beaten
1/2 cup long-grain rice, cooked
raisins or currants

Scald milk, being careful not to let it boil. Remove from the stove and add sugar, stirring well. Slowly add this mixture to the beaten eggs, mixing well. Add rice (and raisins or currants, if desired) and mix thoroughly. Turn into a 1 1/2–quart baking dish and bake in a slow oven (300°) for 45 minutes or until browned. This pudding can be served warm or cold.

Betty's Scandinavian Pudding

Along with Aunt Lydia's salad, Betty's Scandinavian pudding has become a must at our Christmas celebration. Like the salad, Scandinavian pudding is a wonderfully easy-to-make and light dessert, which is particularly good to use after a rich, heavy meal. Actually in my own childhood Christmases we alternated, according to mood, between Princess Charlotte pudding and this one. Both were favorites, and both can be used throughout the year.

1 package unflavored gelatin
1/2 cup cold water
5 eggs, separated (use pasteurized eggs)*
3/4 cup sugar
juice of 1 lemon
1 teaspoon grated lemon rind
pinch of salt

---

* See Food Fact on page 153.

1. Soak gelatin in cold water. Dissolve over boiling water using a double boiler. Cool to lukewarm. In a large mixing bowl, beat egg yolks well. (The key to success in this recipe is to ensure proper firmness by beating the egg yolks until they are thick, creamy, and slightly lightened in color.)

2. Add sugar a little at a time, beating thoroughly after each addition. Add lemon juice and lemon rind and continue beating. Add cooled gelatin mixture and beat again. Add salt to egg whites and beat until stiff. Fold lightly into yolk mixture.

3. Pour into 1 1/2-quart compote bowl. Chill until firm. Top with whipped cream and maraschino cherries or finely ground toasted almonds as garnish.

Chinese Almond Pudding

While I was doing graduate work along with teaching school, I had the privilege of living at the United States home office of Bethel Mission of China. That experience enriched my whole life. Chinese Almond Pudding was a favorite dessert there, as well as at the home of the former governor of Nanking, China, where I often went to Bible studies and regularly took Chinese painting lessons. My recipe for this pudding came from Betty Mayling Hu, vice president, Bethel Mission of China.

1 package unflavored gelatin
1/2 cup cold water
1/3 cup sugar
1/8 teaspoon salt
1 cup boiling water
1 cup condensed milk
1 teaspoon almond extract

1. Sprinkle gelatin on cold water to soften. Add sugar, salt, and boiling water and stir until thoroughly dissolved. Add milk and almond extract. Pour into 10" x 6" dish and chill.

2. To serve: Cut pudding into small squares and serve as almond pudding, or mix with chilled canned fruit cocktail and serve as almond fruit dessert.

Prince Charles Bread Pudding

This particular bread pudding was introduced to the Bullock's Wilshire Tea Room (which became I. Magnin) during a special promotion relating to England. Reportedly it is a longtime favorite of the prince.

16 slices of white bread, cut in quarters
1/2 lb. raisins
1/2 lb. butter (cubed)
4 cups half-and-half
1 tablespoon vanilla
1/2 tablespoon cinnamon
6 eggs, beaten
1 cup sugar

1. Layer the first three ingredients in a large casserole dish. Do several layers. In a separate bowl, thoroughly mix together the remaining ingredients. Evenly pour the wet mixture over the layered ingredients and bake at 350° for 45 minutes or until done.

2. Serve warm with a topping of marmalade and whipping cream.

Princess Charlotte Pudding

1 tablespoon unflavored
   gelatin
6 tablespoons cold water
1 tablespoon cornstarch
6 tablespoons sugar
2 egg yolks
2 cups milk

1 teaspoon vanilla
1/2 pint whipping cream
6 tablespoons
   confectioners' sugar
1/4 cup slivered roasted
   almonds

1. Soften the gelatin in cold water and set aside. Mix sugar and cornstarch together in a heavy saucepan. In a separate bowl, beat the egg yolks. Add milk to the egg yolks and blend thoroughly. Then add this mixture to the sugar mixture. Cook over low flame, stirring constantly, until the mixture has the consistency of heavy cream. Add the softened gelatin and stir until dissolved. Cool. Then chill until the mixture begins to thicken, but do not let it get firm. Whip the cream, adding the confectioners' sugar and vanilla to the mixture as you whip it.

2. Fold the custard mixture and almonds into the whipped cream. Spoon the mixture into one large mold or six individual molds and chill until firm.

3. Unmold and serve with Red Raspberry Sauce.

> ❀ **HELPFUL HINT**
>
> An attractive way to serve Princess Charlotte Pudding is on a large glass plate. Soak sugar cubes in orange extract and place around the plate at about three-inch intervals. Just before bringing the pudding to the table, light the sugar cubes to provide a dramatic entrance.

Red Raspberry Sauce

1 package frozen red raspberries
sugar, to taste
1 teaspoon cornstarch

1. Force the thawed berries through a sieve into a small saucepan to yield approximately 1 cup of juice. Then add sugar to the juice. In a separate dish, mix the cornstarch with a little of the juice and then add this mixture to the saucepan. Cook the mixture over a low flame, stirring constantly, until it is clear and slightly thickened.

2. This sauce can either be poured over the pudding before it served or served separately at the table in a glass pitcher.

Snow Pudding

1 tablespoon unflavored gelatin
1/4 cup cold water
1 cup boiling water
1 cup sugar
1/4 cup lemon juice
1/8 teaspoon grated lemon rind
3 egg whites, stiffly beaten (use pasteurized eggs)*
food coloring (optional)

1. Soften gelatin in cold water and then dissolve in boiling water over a double boiler. Add sugar, lemon juice, and lemon rind. Set aside to cool, stirring occasionally. When the mixture is thick enough to hold the mark of a spoon, beat with a whisk until frothy. Add stiffly beaten egg whites and food coloring, if desired, and continue beating until the mixture holds its own

---

* See Food Fact on page 153.

shape. Refrigerate until ready to serve in individual custard dishes, with a topping of custard sauce.

Custard Sauce

2 cups scalded milk
3 egg yolks
1/4 cup sugar
1/8 teaspoon sea salt
1/4 teaspoon vanilla extract

1. Beat egg yolks slightly. Mix in sugar and salt. Gradually add scalded milk, stirring constantly.

2. Cook in a double boiler, stirring, until the mixture thickens and coats a spoon. Remove from stove, add vanilla, and chill.

Vanilla Chiffon Pudding

This is a simple recipe, versatile enough to use for almost any person and every occasion. It is plain enough to use for someone who has been sick or for a small child, and it also makes an excellent dessert at the end of an elaborate meal. My memories of it go back to Christmas Day dinner when it was served in crystal dishes, topped with chocolate curls.

1 envelope of unflavored gelatin
1/4 cup sugar
2 eggs, separated (use pasteurized eggs)*
1 3/4 cups extra-rich milk
1/4 teaspoon vanilla

In a medium saucepan, combine the gelatin with 2 tablespoons sugar. Mix in the egg yolks beaten together with the milk. Let this mixture stand for a minute. Then stir over low heat until the gelatin is completely dissolved; add vanilla.

---

* See Food Fact on page 153.

2. Transfer the mixture to a large bowl. Chill, stirring occasionally, until the mixture forms slight mounds when dropped from a spoon.

3. In a medium-size bowl, beat the egg whites until the mixture forms soft peaks. Gradually add the remaining sugar. Beat until stiff. Fold this mixture into the gelatin mixture. Divide the mixture into separate dessert dishes and chill until set. Garnish with chocolate curls and/or whipped cream.

This recipe may be used as a pie filling by adding the mixture to a chocolate cookie piecrust.

MAIN DISHES

Chili and Beans

Even though this chili recipe is made totally from scratch, it is not difficult to make and provides a wonderful aroma throughout the house while cooking. This recipe was given to me by my friend Lee Petty, whose family came to California years ago with Father Serra. Lee's grandmother used to grow chilis, dry them in the sun, grind them, and then make her chili sauce. (I suppose by that standard, this recipe is not "totally from scratch"!)

pinto beans	*salt, pepper, garlic powder*
water	*to taste*
1 lb. ground beef	*1 large can chili sauce*
1 medium onion, chopped	

1. Wash pinto beans, 15 to 20 at a time; discard any small rocks and twigs. Put beans into a large, heavy pot. (Use enough beans to cover the bottom of the pan 2"–2 1/2" deep; beans triple in size when they are cooked.)

2. Fill the pot with water. Bring to a boil. Then turn down to low. Cook for several hours until the beans turn pink and are soft to touch. Drain the liquid from the beans and save it.

3. In a large frying pan, brown ground beef, seasoned to taste with salt, pepper, and garlic powder. Add chopped onion. Add mixture to the pot with the beans. Mix in one large can of chili sauce. I sometimes use only 1/2–3/4 of a can, depending on how spicy I want the end result to be. Boil some of the reserved bean water and gradually add it to the mixture until it has the consistency of tomato sauce or thick soup. (Be sure to bring the bean water to a boil first, or it will cause discoloration.) Simmer, stirring occasionally. If more liquid is needed, add boiling bean juice or boiling water.

Note: To *reduce* the amount of liquid, cook it away; to *increase* the liquid, add boiling water or bean juice.

Hint: When I combine the meat mixture with the cooked beans, I find it easier to put the chili and beans into the slow cooker and cook at a low temperature until I am ready to serve it. Chili and beans is an attractive dish when served in earthenware bowls, along with a good cornbread.

Rice: How to Cook Fluffy Rice Chinese Style on American Stoves

This fluffy rice recipe is a good basic way to cook rice in general. It comes from my days of living at Bethel Mission of China and is reprinted from Betty Hu's booklet called *Chinese Recipes*.

1. *Wash rice seven times*—or until water is not cloudy.

2. *Fill pot with cold water,* leaving one inch of water above rice—measure with your index finger this way: while touching the rice with the fingertip, the water level should reach the first bend of your index finger.

3. *Place over hot fire and bring to a boil*—if using an electric stove, you should heat the plate red-hot before placing the rice pot over it.

4. *Stir rice to prevent sticking, turn heat very low, cover tightly and simmer for 20 minutes*—if using electricity, turn off power completely and let pot simmer on plate for 20 minutes. *Do not uncover pot and peek during this period.*

   Your rice is ready to be served piping hot with meat and vegetables!

   Note: Use one handful of rice for each person and an extra handful for the pot.

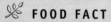 **FOOD FACT**

Basmati rice is a whole grain Indian rice, famous for its nutty aroma. It is more nutritious than white rice and, in my opinion, more tasty than brown rice.

Rice Pilaf

Second only to the potato casserole as an accompaniment to meat dishes is this recipe I got from my friend Marilyn, which I use quite frequently.

3 tablespoons butter
1/2 cup fine egg noodles
1 cup long-grain rice
3 cups chicken broth
1 small can sliced, drained mushrooms, if desired

1. In a large frying pan, melt the butter. Add the noodles and brown them over medium heat. Add the rice and cook until it turns chalky white in color. Add chicken broth. At this point, a small can of sliced mushrooms, drained, may be added if desired.

2. Cover and simmer gently until rice has absorbed all liquid, approximately 20 minutes.

MEAT DISHES

Beef and Broccoli

This recipe comes from my days of living at Bethel Mission of China and is reprinted from Betty Hu's booklet called *Chinese Recipes*. This meat dish is easy to make and nutritious and goes well with fluffy rice and a slice of French bread and/or fresh fruit.

1 round steak or a flank steak

2 bunches of broccoli

2 tablespoons Chinese soy sauce

1 teaspoon sugar

Salt, pepper

2 tablespoons lard or bacon fat (I sometimes substitute
*   2 tablespoons of olive oil.)*

1 tablespoon cornstarch or flour in half a cup of water
*   (I sometimes substitute chicken broth for water.)*

Slivered fresh ginger, if desired

1. Cut beef into thin slices, add salt, pepper, sugar, and soy sauce. Let stand 10 to 20 minutes. Cut broccoli into bite-size pieces. Take off outer rough skin, if you wish.

2. Place one tablespoon of lard into hot pan. Stir beef in, sear quickly, and take meat out. Put the other tablespoon of lard into hot pan and sauté broccoli until done. Use a big flame all the way through, but stir constantly. Add salt, pepper, and water so that steam can go through the vegetable. Thicken gravy with cornstarch and water. Stir in the beef and cook one minute. Then serve with fluffy, hot rice. Serves 6.

Beef and Celery

This recipe comes from my days of living at Bethel Mission of China and is reprinted from Betty Hu's booklet called *Chinese Recipes*. This meat dish is easy to make and nutritious and goes well with fluffy rice and a slice of French bread and/or fresh fruit.

1 round steak or a flank steak
1 stalk celery, or as much as desired
3 tablespoons Chinese soy sauce
1 teaspoon sugar
salt
pepper
2 tablespoons lard or bacon fat (I sometimes substitute
*   2 tablespoons of olive oil.)*
1 tablespoon cornstarch or flour in 1/2 cup of water
*   (I sometimes substitute chicken broth for water.)*
Slivered fresh ginger, if desired

1. Cut beef into thin slices, add salt, pepper, sugar, and soy sauce. Let stand 10 to 20 minutes. Cut celery into thin slices.

2. Place one tablespoon of lard into hot pan. Stir in the beef, sear quickly, and take meat out. Put the other tablespoon of lard into hot pan and sauté celery until done. Use a big flame all the way through, stirring constantly. Add salt, pepper, and water so that steam can go through the vegetable. Thicken gravy with cornstarch and water. Stir in the beef and cook one minute. Then serve with fluffy hot rice. Serves 6.

Chicken Divan

4 frying chicken breasts, halved
water
approximately 3 lb. fresh broccoli
2 tablespoons butter
flour
1 cup chicken broth

1 teaspoon Worcestershire sauce
1 1/4 cups grated mild cheddar cheese
1 cup sour cream, room temperature
salt to taste
paprika

1. Simmer chicken (with skin) in enough water to cover for 25 minutes or just until cooked through. Skin and bone cooked chicken. Cook broccoli and drain. Preheat oven to 325°. Melt butter over low heat in a stainless steel, glass, or enamel saucepan. Stir in flour to thicken, and cook until bubbly. Gradually add broth, stirring constantly, and Worcestershire sauce. Cook, stirring, until thickened.

2. Reduce heat. Stir in 1 cup of the cheese, heating gently until melted. Empty sour cream into a medium-size bowl. Gradually add cheese sauce, stirring constantly. Add salt to taste. Arrange broccoli in 8 portions in a 13" x 9" baking dish. Top each portion with half a chicken breast. Pour sauce over all. Sprinkle with remaining cheese and paprika. Bake 20 minutes or until heated through. Makes 8 servings.

Chicken Tortilla Casserole

1 can cream of mushroom soup
1 can cream of chicken soup
1 cup milk
1 cup green chili salsa
1 onion, minced
1 whole roasting chicken, cooked and cut into small pieces
12 corn tortillas, each torn into 4–6 pieces
1 can sliced black olives
1 pound grated cheddar cheese

Mix the first five ingredients together in a bowl. Grease a 9" x 13" pan. Using half of the ingredients only, layer tortilla pieces, chicken pieces, liquid sauce mixture, olives, and cheese. Repeat layers a second time. Cover with foil and bake at 350° for 45 minutes. Uncover and bake an additional 15 minutes. Serves 8.

This recipe may also be made in two 1 1/8- to 2-quart casserole dishes so that one can be used immediately and one can be frozen for future use. To cook after freezing, thoroughly defrost and then bake as directed.

Lance's Chicken Jambalaya

4 chicken breast halves
1 medium onion, chopped
1 green bell pepper, chopped
1 red pepper, chopped
1 yellow or orange pepper, chopped (optional)

2 tablespoons butter (or margarine)
4 cups rice
hot pepper sauce to taste
Cajun seasoning to taste

1. Boil chicken breasts for approximately an hour in 12 cups of water. While boiling, season generously with pepper sauce and Cajun seasoning. (This isn't a very precise recipe, so don't be afraid to use a little more or less chicken.) Remove chicken when done. Place pieces in freezer until cool enough to handle. Set aside pot with chicken stock.

2. Melt butter or margarine in skillet. Chop the onion and peppers, add to skillet, and sauté. Season generously with hot pepper sauce and Cajun seasoning.

3. Add the peppers and onion to pot in which you boiled the chicken. Remove cooled chicken from freezer. It should be extremely easy to tear the chicken into pieces with your hands. Discard fat and bones. Add shredded chicken to pot.

4. Heat until the stock is boiling. Then add rice, cover, and decrease heat. Remove from heat when most of the stock has been cooked away, but while rice is still moist. Depending on the amount of stock that boiled away while cooking the

chicken, this could take longer than twenty minutes. Add a dash of pepper sauce and Cajun seasoning.

You'll find this will feed seven to eight people. It also makes great leftovers. If you don't want to cook this much, use 2 chicken breasts in 6 cups of water with 2 cups rice. Then reduce the volume of onions and peppers accordingly.

You might also want to substitute shrimp or pork for the chicken.

Jellied Veal (Kalv Sylta)

This is a good recipe to use as an unusual side dish for a buffet or as an hors d'oeuvre, served with crackers. It is very Swedish.

2 lbs. veal shank (approximately)
1 lb. veal shoulder (approximately)

The amount of meat and bones can be increased as desired. With a clean, damp cloth, wipe the meat and bones. Place the meat into a large, heavy pot with:

2 quarts boiling water
1 tablespoon salt
1 medium onion, sliced
10 whole allspice
2 bay leaves
10 peppercorns
dash of pepper

1. Bring the mixture to a boil and skim off the foam. Cover, reduce the heat, and simmer for approximately 2 hours or until the meat is tender. Remove the meat from the broth and cool. Strain the broth and return it to the pot. Boil rapidly, uncovered, until 1 quart of the liquid remains.

2. Remove the meat from the bones. Cut meat into small pieces or put it through the medium blade of a food chopper. Add the

meat to the broth along with 3/4 teaspoon ginger and 1/4 teaspoon pepper. Pour into a 9 1/2" x 5 1/4" x 2 3/4" loaf pan and set aside to cool. Chill in refrigerator until firm. Slice and serve with lemon wedges.

Mushroom Chicken

4 chicken breasts or thighs
1 can cream of mushroom soup
a dash of white wine, if desired
1 can sliced mushrooms (drained)
chopped celery
salt and pepper, and any other desired seasoning

1. Place all ingredients in the slow cooker before leaving the house in the morning. Set the heat to low. Dinner will be ready by evening.

2. Served with steamed rice and a salad or vegetable, or just sliced tomatoes attractively presented on lettuce with a touch of dressing, this meal is nutritious and attractive. A sprig of parsley on the plate, a glass of red cranberry juice, or a hot roll can all be added to the menu according to individual preference. This recipe is readily adaptable for different numbers of people.

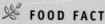 **FOOD FACT**

Many believe that **cranberry juice** is an aid in preventing and treating urinary infections.

Tuna Roll

2 cups flour
1/2 teaspoon salt
4 teaspoons baking powder
1/4 cup shortening
1 egg, beaten
1/2 cup milk
2 cups flaked tuna

1/4 cup milk
2 teaspoons chopped onion
1 1/2 tablespoons chopped parsley
1/2 cup chopped sweet pickle
1/4 teaspoon salt

1. Sift flour with salt and baking powder. Cut in shortening until the mixture resembles coarse crumbs. Add beaten egg and milk. Mix just until dough follows fork around the bowl. On a lightly floured surface, roll out the dough into a rectangular shape, 1/2" thick. In a separate bowl, combine the remaining ingredients. Spread the mixture evenly over the dough. Roll into a jelly roll shape and pinch both ends of dough.

2. Place on a greased cookie sheet and bake in a hot oven (425°) for 20–30 minutes, until golden brown. Slice tuna roll in 1" slices and serve with cheese sauce over each slice.

Cheese Sauce

3 tablespoons butter
3 tablespoons flour
1 1/2 cups milk
1 cup grated cheddar cheese

Melt the butter. Blend in the flour. Gradually add milk and stir over low heat until the mixture is thick. Add grated cheese and stir until melted.

Turkey Meat Loaf

1/4 cup (1/2 stick) butter
2 large onions, finely
 chopped (about 2 cups)
1/4 cup flour
3/4 cup milk
1/2 cup chili salsa
1 teaspoon sea salt
1 teaspoon ground white
 pepper

1 teaspoon dried thyme
3 eggs, well beaten
1/4 cup oatmeal
1/2 cup saltine crackers,
 crushed
3 pounds fresh ground
 turkey

1. Melt butter in a medium skillet over medium heat. Add onions and stir for five minutes. Sprinkle flour over the mixture and stir for one more minute. Slowly add milk, stirring constantly. Mix in chili salsa. Add salt, white pepper, and thyme. Cook mixture for about two minutes or until it is thick and bubbling.

2. Remove skillet from heat and pour the mixture into a bowl. Stir, cool slightly, and refrigerate until chilled.

3. Add chilled mixture to turkey and mix well. Stir in well-beaten eggs. Add oatmeal and crackers and stir well.

4. Divide the mixture, shape into two loaves, and place into two medium-size loaf pans. For freezing, wrap one pan tightly. Bake the other loaf for 50 minutes at 350°. To cook after freezing, thoroughly defrost and then bake as directed.

Yorkshire Pudding

1 cup sifted all-purpose flour
1/2 teaspoon sea salt
2 eggs, well beaten
1 cup milk
1/4 cup hot beef drippings

1. Mix together flour and salt. In a separate bowl combine eggs and milk. Gradually mix eggs and milk into flour mixture and beat until smooth. Heat the beef drippings in a shallow pan. Pour the batter into the hot beef drippings. Bake at 400° for 25–30 minutes.

2. If you wish to bake Yorkshire pudding in the pan with a roast, drain all but 1/4 cup of drippings from the pan about 1/2 hour before the roast is done. Shift the roast to one side of the pan.

3. Pour the batter into the hot drippings and bake, increasing the oven heat to 400°.

4. A plain roast goes well with the more elaborate monkey bread (see recipe on page 142) or a simple Yorkshire pudding. Such a meal could be rounded out by the addition of a simple salad, or by a relish plate that includes olives or celery and carrot sticks, along with something a little more fancy, like canned miniature corncobs or small sweet pickles. Dessert could be simple or elegant, as desired.

> **HELPFUL HINT**
> The perfect garnish to serve with roast beef is a blend of horseradish and whipped cream, mixed in proportions according to taste.

SALADS

Betty's Dessert Salad

This salad is extra rich, as salads go. It is, therefore, a good accompaniment for a simple meat dish and/or a dinner that will be ended with a light dessert.

3 oz. package lime gelatin
2 teaspoons sugar
1 cup boiling water
1/2 cup whipping cream
1/4 cup mayonnaise

1/2 cup chopped walnuts
1 small can crushed
*   pineapple, drained*
3 oz. cream cheese, softened

1. In a small mixing bowl combine the first three ingredients to dissolve gelatin. In a larger bowl, cream the softened cream cheese and mayonnaise and add drained crushed pineapple and nuts. Mix thoroughly.

2. When the gelatin mixture has cooled, gradually add it to the cream cheese mixture, blending thoroughly. Refrigerate until the mixture begins to thicken but not until set. Fold in cream, whipped. Spoon into individual molds and refrigerate until well set. Serve on lettuce leaf, topped with a dab of whipped cream and a maraschino cherry or half a walnut. Serves 4.

Fruit Delight

11 oz. can mandarin
*   orange segments*
1 lb. can pineapple chunks
2 3–oz. packages orange or
*   lemon gelatin*
1 cup boiling water
1 3/4 cup ginger ale

2 3–oz. packages cream
*   cheese*
1/2 cup walnuts (finely
*   chopped)*
honey dressing (recipe
*   below)*

1. Drain the mandarin oranges and the pineapple, reserving 1 cup of syrup. In a large bowl, dissolve the gelatin in boiling water. Add reserved syrup along with the ginger ale. Chill until slightly thickened.

2. Make 24 small balls from the cream cheese. Roll in walnuts and chill. Place the cheese balls in the bottom of a 1 1/8–quart ring mold. Spoon enough of the gelatin mixture over the cheese balls to hold them in place. Refrigerate.

3. Fold the completely drained fruit into the remaining gelatin. Let the mixture stand at room temperature. When gelatin mold is almost set, pour the gelatin and fruit mixture into the mold. Chill until set.

4. When ready to serve, unmold onto a platter and place the honey dressing in a small dish in the center. Serves 8.

Honey Dressing for Fruit Salad

2 tablespoons fresh lemon juice
2 tablespoons honey
1 cup sour cream

Blend juice and honey. Gradually blend in sour cream. Refrigerate several hours to blend flavors. Makes about 1 1/4 cup. This is a low-calorie dressing.

 HELPFUL HINT

When you are going to unmold a gelatin salad on a plate, first add a tiny amount of cold water to the plate. Then if the salad unmolds in the wrong place on the serving plate, it can be shifted easily.

Lydia's Molded Salad

My aunt Lydia's salad has become a tradition at Christmas, but we also use it frequently at various types of dinner parties. It is very tasty and adds variety and color to most meals.

1 package lemon gelatin
1 cup boiling water
1 cup heavy cream,
  whipped
1/2 cup cottage cheese
1 package lime gelatin

1 cup boiling water
1 cup pineapple juice
1 cup crushed pineapple
1/3 cup stuffed olives, sliced
1/3 cup chopped walnuts

1. Dissolve lemon gelatin in boiling water and cool slightly. Beat with eggbeater. Add whipped cream and beat. Add cottage cheese and beat well.

2. Pour into large gelatin mold and let set until quite firm.

3. Dissolve lime gelatin in boiling water and add pineapple juice and remaining ingredients. Pour on top of lemon gelatin mixture and refrigerate until quite firm. Unmold on large glass platter and garnish with lettuce leaves.

✳ HELPFUL HINT

Gelatin has a number of uses. *Aspic jelly* can be made from canned broth and cut into fancy shapes for a garnish. Either vegetables or meat can be molded into the aspic for use as a salad or entrée. To make an aspic jelly pour 1/2 cup stock (such as canned chicken broth) into a bowl, sprinkle with 2 envelopes of unflavored gelatin, and stir thoroughly. In a saucepan heat 3 cups of stock and add 2 tablespoons of lemon juice, the grated rind of one lemon, and 1/2 teaspoon of paprika. Add to first mixture. Add 2 slightly beaten egg whites. Boil for 5 minutes, stirring constantly. Cool, strain, add chopped meat or vegetables if desired, and chill. Chopped pimiento and/or chopped green pepper can add color as well as flavor if the aspic is to be used for a salad or entrée.

HELPFUL HINT

For a last-minute, quick salad, apart from a simple tossed salad or sliced tomatoes, here's one I often use that is simple but still has a look of elegance. It requires a can of pear halves, a 3-oz. pkg. of cream cheese, milk, and, if desired, walnut halves. The cream cheese should be softened with a little milk, and then approximately one tablespoon of the mixture can be stuffed into the groove of each pear half. One or two halves, each topped with half a walnut, set on top of a lettuce leaf, provides a delicious accompaniment to many different kinds of meals, including those that are elaborate. An alternative is to use canned peach halves stuffed with cranberry or lingonberry sauce.

Tomato Aspic

This salad goes well with pork sausage casserole, as well as with other casseroles and meat dishes.

1 package strawberry gelatin
1 cup boiling water
1 cup tomato juice, heated
1 teaspoon vinegar
1 tablespoon grated onion
1 tablespoon chopped celery
1 tablespoon green pepper
1 tablespoon stuffed olives cut in half

1. Dissolve gelatin in boiling water. Add heated tomato juice and vinegar. Chill until partially set.

2. Mix in remaining ingredients and pour into an 8" x 8" glass pan.

3. Refrigerate until set. Cut into squares and serve on lettuce leaf.

SANDWICHES

Finger Sandwiches

For a light afternoon tea, which by definition has a more social emphasis, finger sandwiches are essential. For high tea, which is geared toward providing a fuller meal, regular sandwiches are appropriate. These latter sandwiches could include chicken or tuna.

Of the smaller finger sandwiches there are four basic types, all with potential for certain variations: finely chopped ham mixed with sweet pickle; cucumber; egg salad; and chopped olive rolled with cream cheese.

With the exception of the chopped olive sandwiches, which are rolled, the bread must be thinly sliced and should always be spread with butter, not mayonnaise. As you are making the sandwiches, keep fresh those that are already done by covering them with a clean cloth that has been dipped in cold water and carefully wrung out until almost dry.

Cucumber sandwiches are the most prized of all tea sandwiches. To prepare the cucumbers, first peel them. Then for decoration run a fork lengthwise on all sides. Slice *paper-thin*. Sprinkle the slices with salt, to draw out the water. Squeeze the slices between paper towels in order to ensure crispness. Place two layers of cucumber slices between two slices of lightly buttered bread. Cut off the crusts. Cut into three rectangles, and then into six, if desired.

One of my favorite tea sandwiches is **chopped ham**. I use canned deviled ham, mixed with finely chopped sweet pickle. Mix with just enough mayonnaise to make the mixture adhere, and spread over a lightly buttered slice of bread. Cover with another lightly buttered slice of bread. Trim the crusts and cut into four to eight triangles, depending on the size of the slice of bread and the size sandwich desired. Remember, for afternoon tea you want small, dainty tea sandwiches.

Egg salad sandwiches are made by simply chopping hard-boiled eggs, adding finely chopped celery, seasoning with salt and pepper to taste, and adding a small amount of mayonnaise to create the right consistency for spreading. Once again, spread between two buttered slices of bread and cut into desired shapes.

Cream cheese and chopped olive sandwiches are made by finely chopping black olives and mixing them with cream cheese softened with milk. Spread the mixture on unbuttered slices of bread that have already been trimmed. Roll each slice and wrap tightly in waxed paper. Chill thoroughly. Before serving, slice each roll into pinwheel-type sandwiches. The sandwiches should be about 1/2" thick. Once the sandwiches are made, store them in a tightly covered container and refrigerate.

In addition to the more traditional tea sandwich, our family has always used a creation of my mother's called a *mandarin orange/ brown bread* tea sandwich. To make these, purchase canned brown bread and canned mandarin orange slices. Slice the bread and spread each slice somewhat thickly with softened cream cheese. Cut in half. Drain the orange slices, cut each orange slice in half, and place on a paper towel to drain. Place one slice on each half-slice of brown bread. These sandwiches should be prepared shortly before serving, although they can be kept in the refrigerator for several hours if they are put in a tightly covered container.

SOUPS

Stone Soup / Chicken Soup

When I know that I'm going to be gone all day, I start this soup the night before by putting chicken bones in the slow cooker to cook all night. The next morning I add vegetables and chicken meat, and let the soup simmer all day, knowing that a pot of hearty soup will welcome me home.

Remember: stone soup is a soup of leftovers.

1 or 2 small chicken
   carcasses or half a
   turkey carcass
water
seasonings, to taste:
salt and pepper
poultry seasoning
Lawry's seasoning
peppercorns
celery tops
3 bay leaves

2–3 chicken bouillon cubes
1/2 cup uncooked rice
1 small can tomato paste
chopped celery
chopped onions
sliced carrots or any other
   leftover vegetables
seasonings, to taste
small amount of leftover
   cut-up chicken or turkey

1. At night, put chicken or turkey carcasses in the slow cooker and fill with water. Add salt, pepper, poultry seasoning, Lawry's seasoning, peppercorns, bay leaves, celery tops, chicken bouillon cubes. Cook all night on the low setting.

2. In the morning take out the bones and celery; skim off the fat. Add uncooked rice, tomato paste, chopped celery and onions, sliced carrots, seasonings to taste, and leftover cut-up chicken or turkey. (I usually keep several cups of chicken frozen for use in soups, casseroles, or sandwiches.) Again, turn on the slow cooker and cook the soup (at the low setting) all day.

You can add barley or pasta instead of rice, freshly chopped tomatoes, green onions, and almost any leftover vegetables.

Another variation of Stone Soup is to separate out some broth, or to use a regular chicken broth bought in the store, and add in a well-beaten egg or two, which will ultimately resemble the egg in the Chinese Egg Flower Soup. Seaweed, which is higher in potassium than almost any other food, can be bought in thin, dried sheets, *slightly* toasted in a pan for a few *seconds*, and added to the soup in small pieces. For anyone who is ill and having difficulty eating anything solid, this soup can have great nutritional value. For anyone else, it is a good pick-me-up.

 HELPFUL HINT

Simmering poultry, meat, fish (and/or their bones), or vegetables can produce stock or broth from which various soups, sauces, and casseroles can be made. Stock can be frozen in blocks, or even in ice cube trays, and used as needed. My favorite is poultry stock made from chicken or turkey, using the whole bird or just bones. Cook the poultry or bones overnight as for stone soup. (In making stock, as opposed to soup, carrots, parsley, celery, onions, and leeks are the best vegetables to use.) Then discard all bones, vegetables, and spices. Cool and refrigerate. After the stock is cold, the fat will solidify on the top and can be skimmed off. Strain, if desired. In order to reduce the stock and thus intensify the flavor, boil at a fast rate until the volume is decreased sufficiently. Adding poultry or beef cubes can also be used to add flavor. When soup or stock is frozen and then defrosted, it should be brought to a rolling boil before using in order to kill harmful bacteria. Bones for stone soup and for broth can be frozen for about six months in a freezer bag. Add bones as you have them available, being careful to tightly reseal the bag each time.

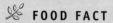 **FOOD FACT**

Researcher Dr. Marvin Sackner, pulmonary specialist at Mount Sinai Medical Center in Miami Beach, concluded: "'There's an aromatic substance in **chicken soup**, not yet identified, that helps clear your airways.' He meticulously measured the effects of cold water, hot water, and chicken soup on the rate of flow of mucus and airflow through nasal passages. . . . Hot water cleared congestion in airways better than cold water, but best of all was hot chicken soup. Even cold chicken soup worked to a lesser extent." (Jean Carper, *Food Pharmacy* [New York: Bantam, 1988], 106.)

 HELPFUL HINT

Another use for gelatin is to make a *jellied soup*. Such a soup used to be popular. Now it is unusual enough to make any dinner party unique, but it is still very simple to make. For a chicken flavor, pour 1/2 cup of cold water into a bowl and sprinkle 2 envelopes unflavored gelatin on top. Add 3 cups hot chicken broth and stir until the gelatin is dissolved. Add 1/4 teaspoon salt, 1/4 teaspoon celery salt, one tablespoon lemon juice, and 1/4 teaspoon poultry powder. Pour into individual bouillon cups that have first been rinsed with cold water. Chill. Jellied soup should have a soft consistency as compared with the firmer consistency of aspic jelly. Before serving beat slightly with a fork. Lemon slices make a good garnish. Chicken broth is best used if a light colored soup is desired. For a richer soup, beef stock can be used. These soups do not have to be chilled. They can also be served hot as a simple soup or broth.

VEGETABLES

Baked Potato Supreme

This recipe is a favorite of mine because it is quick, nutritious, and open to variation. It can effectively be used for breakfast, lunch, or dinner, particularly if it is served with fresh fruit. Vegetables, meats, different cheeses, and a variety of other possibilities can make this dish different and suited to individual tastes. I have chosen to eliminate sour cream, minimize cheddar cheese, and emphasize cottage cheese in order to reduce fat and calories and increase nutrition.

Using 1 medium to large size baking potato, scrub the skin well with a brush. Pierce the skin with a fork in several places. Microwave on high for 6–8 minutes, or until done, or bake in a conventional oven. Cut and squeeze the potato as if preparing to serve it as a simple baked potato. Add several tablespoons of cottage cheese, sprinkle with shredded cheddar cheese according to taste, and top with chopped green onion or bacon bits. Microwave on high until cheese is melted and bubbly. Baked Potato Supreme can be made early in the day and then microwaved for about 2 minutes, or until cheese is soft and bubbly, before serving.

✿ FOOD FACT

A **baked potato** contains only about 115 calories. It is high in fiber, minerals, and vitamin C as well as other vitamins. Along with cantaloupe, avocados, bananas, oranges, soybeans, and peanuts, baked potatoes are high in potassium. Many experts feel that potatoes help prevent strokes. What you add to the potato can increase its nutritional value, but be careful of adding too much fat and too many calories.

Vegetable Terrine

Vegetable terrine is delicious served hot or cold, and actually tastes better if it is made a day ahead. Then for the sanity of the host or hostess, as well as the waistlines and digestive systems of the guests, after choosing a couple of elaborate dishes it is good to make the rest of the dinner more simple.

2 pounds carrots, peeled
  and sliced
4 tablespoons butter
1/2 pound mushrooms,
  sliced
1 pound fresh spinach,
  without stems
4 eggs
1/2 cup half-and-half

3/4 cup freshly shredded
  Parmesan cheese
1/2 cup shredded cheddar
  cheese
3/4 cup shredded
  mozzarella cheese
1/2 teaspoons sea salt
1/2 teaspoon pepper
pinch of nutmeg

Steam the carrots until tender. Chop coarsely and put in a large mixing bowl. Sauté mushrooms in 3 tablespoons butter. Chop coarsely and add mushrooms to carrots. Sauté spinach in 1 tablespoon butter until tender. Set aside. Beat eggs, half-and-

---

✳ HELPFUL HINT

Choosing fresh vegetables can be a challenge. Here are some hints: Lettuce should not be hard or the taste may be bitter. A little give in its feel indicates sweeter flavor. Celery that is lighter green in color will also have a sweeter flavor. Cucumbers have smaller seeds when they are long and thin. Avocados make a tasty, nutritious addition to a tossed salad. Once an avocado is cut or peeled, however, it quickly becomes discolored. To prevent this, sprinkle lemon juice over the avocado. An additional hint: be sure to tear lettuce rather than cut it, to avoid unsightly browning. Chives, on the other hand, are best cut with scissors.

half, and cheeses. Combine with the carrots and mushrooms. Add seasonings. Heavily butter a 9" x 4" x 3" baking pan. Fill with half the carrot mixture. Evenly spread the spinach over the carrot mixture and add the remaining carrot mixture. Place the loaf pan in a pan of water and

bake in a preheated oven at 400° for 45–60 minutes, or until set. Remove from the oven and let it rest for 15 minutes. Unmold onto a heated platter and serve warm, or keep refrigerated up to three days and serve cold or reheated. This dish may also be frozen and then reheated. Serves at least 8.

Vegetable Accompaniment

(looks elaborate, but is very simple)

1 package of frozen, blunt cut string beans
1 small carton of sour cream
1 can of cut-up mushrooms, sautéed

Immediately after cooking the beans, pour off any liquid from the pan and quickly stir in the carton of sour cream and the sautéed mushrooms. Transfer into a serving bowl immediately or the texture may become curdled.

✿ ADDITIONAL FOOD FACTS
AND HELPFUL HINTS

The flavor and texture of **hot chocolate** will be greatly enhanced if you beat the mixture with a hand beater or blender rather than just mixing the ingredients with a spoon.

To remove **fish odors** from plates, dishcloths, etc., soak them for a short time in a solution of water and baking soda (1 to 2 teaspoons baking soda to one quart of water). To remove odors from a refrigerator, leave an open box of baking soda on one of the middle shelves.

Read **labels** if you are concerned about what you are eating. Remember, ingredients are listed according to the amount present—starting with the highest amount first and going to the lowest amount last. Be sure to read *all* of the ingredients. For example, sometimes you may find that when fat levels are lowered in a cheese product, the sodium level is increased. Also, words like *lean, lite,* and *light* may not refer to fat at all—they can simply mean lighter color or even just fewer calories (as in drinks). As a further example, "no cholesterol" means just that. It does not mean that the product is fat-free. In the same way, *unsalted* or *no salt added* or *without added salt* means that salt normally added is not present, but that the normal amount of sodium contained in the food still exists. Only when a product says "sodium-free" can you be sure of its sodium level—less than 5 mg. per serving. Keep in mind that sodium is measured in milligrams. Therefore, when a product is advertised as containing less than one *gram*, the salt content may still be very high.

Legislation has been passed to require more accurate and complete labeling of food products. Until that totally takes effect, it is essential for the consumer to understand as clearly as possible what he or she is reading on any given food label. Once you have been able to determine what is contained in a product, a generally accepted rule of thumb relating to the amount of fat, salt, and sugar in a food is to avoid total deprivation. If you love french fries, don't say, "I'll never have another french fry again." Set an allowable amount for yourself—e.g., one order of french fries each week or month. This will help avoid the kind of craving that inevitably leads to bingeing.

Many who must cut down on **salt** because of high blood pressure do not always realize common sources of "hidden" salt. For example, one cup of tomato juice contains about 880 mg. of sodium! Fortunately, low-sodium tomato juice is readily available in the market. A small can of V-8, which to me is a tasty replacement for tomato juice, contains only 95 mg. of sodium and is rich in potassium (620 mg.). Again, read the label, since different types of V-8 have different levels of sodium, potassium, etc.

Sea salt does not contain sodium chloride only. Instead, it balances sodium with other seawater minerals. In contrast, common household salt is processed with various additives and has a flat taste.

Seafood is a wonderful source of vitamin D, which may help prevent calcium loss. Canned salmon and canned sardines both have three to five times as much vitamin D as a cup of milk. Even though fish can be fatty, compared to other foods the fat level is still relatively low. Furthermore, certain fish oils considerably reduce the risk of heart attack.

For calming **snacks** or munch breaks try: unsalted popcorn, unsalted dry-roasted peanuts, unsalted almonds, raisins, cubes of hard cheese, salt-free peanut butter spread on salt-free wheat crackers, sugar-free yogurt, apples, bananas or other fruit in season.

Nuts are a good source of protein for a mid-afternoon snack. They are high in fat and in calories, but they do not contain cholesterol; and most fat contained in nuts is unsaturated.

Tryptophan is an amino acid that is important in helping to regulate moods and sleep patterns. It is involved in the production of serotonin, which affects mood chemistry. Good sources of tryptophan are bananas, beef liver, beef round, lamb, turkey, eggs, almonds, peanuts, and milk. In contrast, alcohol seems to decrease the levels of tryptophan in the body, a fact that may account for alcohol-induced depression. (Harvey M. Ross and June Roth, *The Mood-Control Diet* [New York: Prentice Hall, 1990], 63.)

Soybeans provide one of nature's complete plant proteins. Soy flour contains twice the amount of protein found in wheat flour. Soy flour, bean sprouts, and tofu (bean curd) are all readily available. The flour can be used to enrich bread, as in some of the bread recipes in this book. The sprouts are delicious in salads or sandwiches. Bean curd can be cut into cubes and cooked lightly with vegetables and/or meat or chicken in a wok—add a taste of fresh ginger and a splash of soy sauce for flavor.

In her excellent book *Fight Fat After Forty*, Pamela Peeke, M.D., M.P.H., states the problem which the Duchess probably faced when she found the need for **afternoon tea**. "The problem begins around 3 to 4 P.M. At that time, the stress hormones are at approximately half their morning level, and most people are beginning to feel tired, as if they are losing their edge. This is the beginning of the CortiZone, when a woman begins to feel very vulnerable to stress eating. The CortiZone extends all the way through midnight. But it is often how a woman handles the beginning of the CortiZone that establishes how she will handle it later." I would add that some of these same problems occur with men.

While at times tea and sweets can provide the safety zone feeling of comfort and hospitality, sometimes we have to eat wisely in order to be and feel more fit.

Adding scientific research to the equation, Dr. Peeke provides more specific information on what foods help when sound nutrition is vital to physical well-being. "Combinations of protein and carbohydrates are ideal. This includes low-fat or fat-free yogurt or cottage cheese, along with a piece of fruit." (Pamela Peeke, M.D., M.P.H., *Fight Fat After Forty* [New York: Viking Penguin, 2000], 104-105, 120.)

Certain **vegetables** seem to have unusually great health value. Broccoli has been called an anti-cancer agent as well as a deterrent to high blood pressure, among other things. Raw onions are thought by some to raise the good cholesterol (HDL) levels and thus help the cardiovascular system. A good rule of thumb is to eat ample amounts of vegetables, as well as fruits, and to stress variety.

A good and healthful way to cook fresh vegetables is to steam them. The simplest way to steam is to buy an inexpensive steamer basket. Rinse the vegetables in cold water and cut up as desired. Fill a pan with about 2 inches of water and bring to a boil. Put the vegetables in the basket and place over the water, not in it or touching it. Cover. Reduce heat and steam until done. Timing varies. For example, spinach takes 6 to 8 minutes while cut-up broccoli takes 13 to 18 minutes. Carrots take 13 to 25 minutes. Test with a fork to check doneness.

After being steamed, certain vegetables like broccoli or carrots can be pureed in a blender. The result will be a fluffy, plain vegetable whose flavor seems enhanced by the blending process and which adds a colorful, simple, nutritional touch to an otherwise rich meal. This is also a good way to prepare vegetables for young children or for invalids who might not be getting enough nutritional value from what they are able to eat.

Yogurt is made by bacteria that change milk by fermentation. These bacteria produce certain byproducts that fight disease. In essence yogurt is nature's antibiotic. However, keep in mind that heating yogurt in cooking will kill these bacteria.

FOODS THAT DO NOT FREEZE WELL	
Food	**Change that Occurs During Freezing**
Breaded and fried foods	Both become soggy.
Buttermilk, yogurt, custard, cottage cheese	These dairy products separate into solids and liquids.
Cake, with custard and pudding fillings	Cake becomes soggy as filling separates into solids and liquid.
Cream cheese	Texture becomes dry and crumbly.
Eggs 　Hard-cooked 　In shell	 White becomes tough and rubbery. Shells crack; yolks are unstable.
Frostings, boiled	Surface becomes weepy.
Gelatin	Surface becomes weepy.
Mayonnaise	Oil separates from solids.
Meats, cured	Salt and fat cause poor freezing and result in quick rancidity.
Potatoes, white, boiled	Texture becomes mealy.
Poultry, stuffed at home	Dressing may not freeze quickly enough to prevent bacteria from multiplying rapidly.
Salad greens, cucumbers, radishes	Crisp vegetables become limp.

(Charles Gerras, ed., *Rodale's Basic Natural Foods Cookbook* [Emmaus, Penn.: Rodale Press, 1984], 757.)

FREEZER STORAGE TIME FOR FISH AND POULTRY

FOOD	Maximum Storage (in months)
Fish:	
Codfish, flounder, haddock, halibut, pollack	6
Mullet, ocean perch, sea trout, striped bass	3
Ocean perch (Pacific)	2
Salmon steak	2
Sea trout, dressed	3
Striped bass, dressed	3
Whiting, drawn	4
Dungeness crab	3
King crab	10
Shrimp	12
Poultry	
Chicken	
Cut-up	9
Livers	3
Whole	12
Duck, whole	6
Goose, whole	6
Turkey	
Cut-up	6
Whole	12

(Charles Gerras, ed., *Rodale's Basic Natural Foods Cookbook* [Emmaus, Penn.: Rodale Press], 756.)

Chapter 1. That Means She Loves Us

1. James Moffatt, D.D., *The New Testament: A New Translation* (New York and London: Harper & Brothers, 1935), 323.

CHAPTER 2. The Safety Zone of Hospitality

1. Carol Rittner and Sondra Myers, eds., *The Courage to Care* (New York: New York University Press, 1986), 23.

2. *Courage,* 20.

3. Laura Ingalls Wilder, *Little House in the Big Woods* (New York: Harper and Row, 1971), 37–39, 42.

4. Personal interview with Ruth Bell Graham, 1990.

5. From John Pollock, *A Foreign Devil in China* (Minneapolis: Worldwide Publications, 1971), 158.

6. P. D. James, *A Taste for Death* (New York: Alfred A. Knopf, 1986), 203.

CHAPTER 3. Given to Hospitality

1. Amy Carmichael, *His Thoughts Said . . . His Father Said* (Fort Washington, Penn.: Christian Literature Crusade), 32.

2. Charles Haddon Spurgeon, *Sermons of Rev. C. H. Spurgeon,* vol. 2 (New York: Funk and Wagnalls, 1857): 93–95.

CHAPTER 4. The Gift of Hospitality

1. Jamieson, Fausset, and Brown, *Critical and Experimental Commentary,* vol. 2 (Grand Rapids: Eerdmans, 1945): 201–202.

2. R. F. Weymouth, D. Lit., *The New Testament in Modern Speech* (London: James Clarke and Co., 1914), 624.

3. James Strong, *The Exhaustive Concordance of the Bible* (New York: Abingdon Press, 1890).

4. Helmut Thielicke and John W. Doberstein, trans., *Encounter with Spurgeon* (Grand Rapids: Baker Book House, 1975), 21.

CHAPTER 5. The Beauty of Simplicity

1. C. S. Lewis, *The Four Loves* (New York: Harcourt Brace Jovanovich, 1960), 126.

CHAPTER 6. A Touch of Elegance

1. Eva Schloss and Evelyn J. Kent, *Eva's Story: A Survivor's Tale by the Sister of Anne Frank* (New York: St. Martin, 1989), 209.

CHAPTER 9. I Love Coffee, I Love Tea

1. Miep Gies, *Anne Frank Remembered* (New York: Simon and Schuster, 1987), 238.

2. *Anne Frank,* 138–139.

3. Catherine Calvert, *Having Tea* (New York: Clarkson N. Potter, Inc., 1987), 15–17.

4. Helen Simpson, *The London Ritz Book of Afternoon Tea* (New York: Arbor House, 1986), 15–17.

5. Noah Adams, *Saint Croix Notes* (Boston: Houghton Mifflin Co., 1990), 58.

RECIPE SECTION

1. Devin Adair, *The Original White House Cookbook* (New York: The Saalfield Publishing Co., l987), 240.

2. James Beard, *Delights & Prejudices* (New York: Atheneum, 1986), 39–40.

✳ RECIPE INDEX